DOING BUSINE

How To Books on business and management

Arranging Insurance
Be a Freelance Sales Agent
Buy & Run a Shop
Buy & Run a Small Hotel
Cash from Your Computer
Collecting a Debt
Communicate at Work
Conduct Staff Appraisals
Conducting Effective Interviews
Conducting Effective Negotiations
Dealing with Your Bank
Doing Business Abroad
Do Your Own Advertising
Do Your Own PR
Employ & Manage Staff
Investing in People
Investing in Stocks & Shares
Keep Business Accounts
Manage a Sales Team
Manage an Office
Manage Computers at Work
Manage People at Work
Managing Budgets & Cash Flows
Managing Credit

Managing Meetings
Managing Yourself
Market Yourself
Master Book-Keeping
Master Public Speaking
Mastering Business English
Organising Effective Training
Prepare a Business Plan
Publish a Book
Publish a Newsletter
Raise Business Finance
Sell Your Business
Start a Business from Home
Start Your Own Business
Starting to Manage
Successful Mail Order Marketing
Taking on Staff
Understand Finance at Work
Use the Internet
Winning Presentations
Write a Report
Write & Sell Computer Software
Writing Business Letters

Other titles in preparation

The How To series now contains more than 200 titles in the following categories:

Business Basics
Family Reference
Jobs & Careers
Living & Working Abroad
Student Handbooks
Successful Writing

Please send for a free copy of the latest catalogue for full details (see back cover for address).

BUSINESS BASICS

DOING BUSINESS ABROAD

How to start trading successfully in international markets

David Horchover

How To Books

This book is dedicated to my wife, Shirley

Cartoons by Mike Flanagan

British Library Cataloguing in Publication Data
A catalogue record for this book is available from the British Library.

© Copyright 1997 by David Horchover.

First published in 1997 by How To Books Ltd, 3 Newtec Place,
Magdalen Road, Oxford, OX4 1RE, United Kingdom.
Tel: (01865) 793806. Fax: (01865) 248780.

Note: The material contained in this book is set out in good faith for
general guidance and no liability can be accepted for loss or expense
incurred as a result of relying in particular circumstances on statements
made in this book. The law and regulations may be complex and liable to
change, and readers should check the current position with the relevant
authorities before making personal arrangements.

Produced for How To Books by Deer Park Productions.
Typeset by Concept Communications (Design & Print) Ltd, Crayford, Kent.
Printed and bound by Cromwell Press, Broughton Gifford, Melksham, Wiltshire.

Contents

List of Illustrations

Note

The forms reproduced in this book have been reduced to fit into book format and are intended to help the reader become familiar with the appearance of the documentation they are likely to need.

It is wise to check that you are using the most up-to-date and current documentation as forms do change from time to time.

Out of date forms will not be accepted and will cause you aggravation and frustration when rejected.

Preface

No business can afford to embark on any venture unless it is reasonably assured of adequate returns. Equally, no business involved in international trade – importing or exporting – should become involved in these activities if there is a risk of exhausting its limited capital, material or manpower. International trading can be both profitable and fun if properly understood, and the lessons learned are correctly applied.

Many organisations have commented that international trade, especially exporting is not for them. The perception is that the procedures involved, such as searching for markets, finding agents, getting paid, handling paperwork and so on are all too complex. *Doing Business Abroad* discredits these myths and replaces them with the essential facts.

Like any business discipline, international trade has its own rules, regulations, systems and methods which have to be understood and adopted if the business is to succeed. This book takes the reader step-by-step through each aspect of exporting and importing, so that prospective traders can assess if and how they can profitably increase the size of their business by engaging in overseas activities.

Following the advice contained here will dispel any fears and doubts you may have about international trade so that you too can participate and succeed in an expanding global market.

I am grateful to David Russell and his colleagues at Frazer International freight forwarders for their help and courtesy in providing documentation, and for their encouragement during the writing of this book. My thanks go also to Sandy who deciphered my almost illegible handwriting and typed the original typescript.

Acknowledgements

The author would like to thank the following organisations for kind permission to reproduce copyright or sponsored material for this book:
The London Chamber of Commerce and Industry, SITRO, HM Customs and Excise, and to Frazer International for supplying the forms in the first place.

1
Exporting

GETTING STARTED

No business can realistically afford to embark on any new venture or activity unless it is reasonably sure that adequate benefits or returns will result. In addition, the business will have to be reassured that, by becoming involved with customers, agents and/or distributors overseas, which is what export is really all about, it will not exhaust the limited capital, material and manpower of the company.

Doing the groundwork

Before exporting is even contemplated, six questions should be answered:

1. Why should a small business export?

2. What can your company export?

3. To whom should you export?

4. How can the goods best be exported?

5. How can your organisation make money from exporting?

6. How can your company guard against failure?

This book will help you to answer all these questions and more. However first let us examine why a small business should consider going into export.

Recognising your potential as a small business

There has never been a better time for small business to become involved in export. There are two reasons for this:

1. There has been a significant change taking place in world trade. There is a movement away from mass production (*ie* providing the greatest quantity of goods at the lowest possible cost for the greatest number of consumers) and the resulting standardisation of products. Consumers are seeking more individual or local products which small businesses are able to provide.

2. There is a growing trend towards 'doing things for yourself' (*ie* DIY) which has led to the demand for more specialised products and personalised services which have traditionally been the forte of the small business.

Other reasons why a small business should contemplate going into export are:

● Export *can* be more rewarding than home-based business in terms of profit – or what should more accurately be described as contribution to revenue. However, no company should expand into export unless it is *certain* or *determined* that the venture will be profitable. This presupposes that the costing and pricing are both right.

● For an increasing number of small exporters the satisfaction of winning overseas business is often just as important as the potential financial rewards.

● One of the major disadvantages of larger companies is that often they are unable to react very quickly to changes in overseas markets. Smaller companies, on the other hand, are able to spot trends or changes in markets and react rapidly.

● Spreading the risk of business will also feature highly in the list of reasons for exporting, for when a company sells or markets in one country, it could be subjected to fluctuations in the fortunes of that country – but not all countries thrive or decline simultaneously. It is therefore wise or prudent to spread the risk so that it stands less chance of suffering when perhaps the domestic market is having a difficult time.

● There is always the worry or danger of a small business becoming complacent in its own home market. Experience proves that by being exposed to what competitors are doing in other parts of the world, a company can often find new ways of doing business of which it may have been unaware.

Using financial resources
Finance or the lack of it should be no deterrent to the would-be exporter. There is an extensive range of sources of finance now available for the smaller business which will be discussed in Chapter 6.

Considering manpower
Having no-one in the company with export experience should not debar companies from exporting. This could in fact be turned to advantage because instead of having separate domestic and export staff, the export business can be incorporated into the existing home trade.

Don't be deterred
Do not believe that exporting is complicated or difficult. Some people may make it seem so. With the information included in this book, you will discover much of what you need to know. If you need more help, then there are many outside sources who can provide it, sometimes free but more usually on a fee-paying basis.

Making a commitment
Never export because the chairman's wife wants to travel overseas or because it is seen to be a good thing to do. *Never* export on a casual basis – take exporting seriously. There must be top **management commitment** to exporting – not just at the time the decision was made to export but on an ongoing basis. If commitment from the top is absent, then the exporting process and success will suffer. Never merely use export for shipping out surplus production because this means that the domestic market will always control exports, which is an activity in its own right.

Questions and answers
Before you begin to export ask yourself the following questions:

What business are we in?
Determine exactly what your business is *capable of achieving*. A cask maker saw demand for his wooden casks decline and his business disappear. He should have looked to see what else he could have made out of wood *eg* toys or furniture, as his skills lay in handling wood.

What is our special expertise – is it manufacturing, selling or innovating?
Some may say all three but smaller companies will tend to excel in one

only. This means that the export objective should be to concentrate on that one. For example, Japanese companies contend that manufacturing is much more effective when it is separated from selling, so, much of their worldwide success has been due to having organisations which manufacture goods sold to their sales subsidiaries.

Which countries do we know best?
Start exporting to countries you already know by way of holidays, school study or reading. You may also include countries you just like – you will tend to be more effective if you empathise with the country you're dealing with.

It might be a good idea to concentrate on parts of the world where you are known, either through friends, relatives or business acquaintances. The maxim: 'It's not *what* you know but *who* you know' is universal.

DECIDING WHAT YOU NEED TO KNOW

If you can provide good reasons for entering the export market, then you will have to seriously ask:

● What do we need to know?

The simplistic answer to this question is: you need to know and appreciate the *minimum necessary* to avoid making potentially costly mistakes. Sadly it is an economic fact that most research produces no tangible results in terms of bankable revenue so, as a small business, you will be unable to afford to spend much time or money on it. On the other hand, nor must you ignore research altogether, as failure to 'find out' could result in the collapse of your business later if not sooner. It is important to get the balance right.

Case studies

Case 1
A French firm set up a timber mill in East Africa. It was about to begin operations when the French realised that there was nowhere near enough electrical power in the region to run the mill. Probably there will never be. The plant had to be dismantled.

Case 2
A British firm returned a consignment of US-made motors believing that

they had not received what they thought they had ordered. Reason: In the UK a right-handed motor in an English mill (where they were to be used) is considered a left-handed motor in the US. *Note*: In the US production is looked at from downstream and so they see the motor in an opposite manner than do the British.

DOING ADEQUATE RESEARCH

Research into markets abroad will not *guarantee* success. What research *will* do is to produce facts about *what* is being bought or *why* particular products are popular. Research will also ascertain the general economic conditions in the parts of the world you are aiming to trade in. This is most important as there is little point in exporting to countries where there are distribution, legal or payment problems (either self-imposed or by government regulations).

Note: Research cannot forecast what is likely to happen in the future. Research, properly carried out, can only reveal facts and attitudes (quantitative and qualitative research).

Interpreting the data

Having been presented with marketing data, you will still need to make the decision as to what should be done. Correct interpretation of marketing data, in itself not always easy, will only help you **reduce the risk of failure, not guarantee success abroad**.

Looking at what you need to know

● You will need to gather basic information about the world as a market-place (would you go on holiday abroad without checking out the area?).

● You will need to know the 'new' names of countries *eg* Myanamar (Burma) and the independent countries of former unions *eg* USSR, Yugoslavia. Knowledge of the ports, climates and distances, will all give you a good idea of where people live, what they do and why, and therefore their style of living.

● You will need to have some idea of the politics of countries to which you are considering exporting as there will usually be regions, territories or countries into which it will be impossible to sell *eg* Libya, Iraq, because of government or international embargoes or restrictions.

- You will need to know whether there are tariff barriers, customs duties, quotas affecting your products.

- You should also check out whether the importing countries have any currency restrictions imposed by their government which means that they cannot pay in sterling (to save their foreign currency reserves).

- It will pay you to investigate which are rich or poor countries, developing or developed countries. For example, where would you place South Korea or Taiwan or the Philippines and Indonesia on the economic scale? One good rule of thumb is to check the electricity output per million people (figures can easily be discovered through the Department of Trade and Industry's Country Desk) as this reflects fairly accurately the development and prosperity of a country.

- Naturally you will check the competition you are likely to meet, not just from the UK but also from elsewhere, classified by quantity and value. You should also find out what is made locally in your product group – to what standard, range and price.

- Currency will feature strongly on your list of what you need to know. Check on its sterling value, its stability and its convertibility.

- Social conditions are usually the most difficult to research and information on these is difficult to obtain as it affects your customers and their buying behaviour.

Checking social conditions

- *Language* (or as in Malaysia, languages) – in Malaysia, Indian, Chinese, Malay and English are all official languages. In Singapore, although the bulk of the population is of Chinese origin and the balance is Malay and Indian, English is the common language.

- *Literacy* – a lack of literacy may demand the use of graphics or images to communicate messages or instructions.

- *Religious differences* could make the selling of alcohol in Muslim countries impossible, pork products will not sell in Jewish territories and money lending is outlawed in Muslim countries – at least in the form the West recognises.

- *The habits and styles* of living within countries should be carefully noted. In some countries, for example, wealth is concentrated in the hands of just a few families who then control what is imported and sold.

Some of these points may seem obvious but it is all too easy to apply what you already know about your own domestic market to the countries to which you are aiming to sell. As a small or first time exporter, you will probably only need to acquire information in relatively few countries, but the data gathered and analysed will be invaluable. If you spend time assessing markets on the basis of what has been outlined, you will be in a better position to know what to sell, and where.

Case studies

Case 1
A company sent expensive sales literature and specifications to a prospect in Brazil – in *Spanish*! The company totally overlooked the fact that *Portuguese* is Brazil's language. Not only was this an embarrassing and avoidable error, it also damaged trade relations before any business had been conducted.

Case 2
Crest toothpaste initially failed in Mexico because the company used an existing campaign based on 'scientifically tested' properties of the product – properties which meant little or nothing to a typical Mexican user.

Case 3
Baby food sold in glass jars in West Africa depicting a baby's head on the wraparound label failed to sell because prospects thought that is what the contents were! The label was changed and sales took off.

Case 4
Sales of a successful canned beer suddenly plummeted in Central Africa. The reason was that the can size and shape were altered and the new cans could not be used as oil lamps or for storage purposes!

CHECKLIST FOR EXPORTERS

- Can you make enough of the product?

- Can you make the product to the specification required (to suit climate, use, storage, transport, shelf-life *etc*)?

- Does your product have an edge over the competition – is the difference big or good enough for it to succeed over the competition?

- Is the product simple to use or is it complicated to construct, fit, get to work or control?

- Does your product need servicing – if so, who *will* or *can* service it?

- Does your product comply with local laws and regulations?

- Will your product need to be protected by a patent or trade mark and how can you check for copying or infringements?

- Will the materials used in the manufacture of your product be acceptable in the destination country? This could even apply, in some instances, to countries where your goods are just in transit.

- Have you checked the size, design, colour of your product, packaging *etc* to avoid gaffes or even to take advantage of preferences? For example, poorer countries have fewer cars and so shoppers may not be able to carry multiple packs, or prefer to buy cigarettes in ones and twos because of cost.

- While in some countries it may be impossible to sell because of religious 'differences', in others, if you can get the approval for what you are selling, then you are already on the road to success. This happens in Ireland where the local parish priest carries a great deal of clout.

These checklist points should be easy enough to research. The information gathered will give you a good idea about the type of market you are aiming to sell into. There will always be surprises and changes, however, which you should be ready to accept and adapt to.

CONSIDERING THE ARGUMENTS AGAINST EXPORTING

Don't imagine that the data gathered so far will be enough for you to make a final decision – one way or the other. While there are plenty of good reasons *for* exporting, there are also perfectly valid arguments *against*. Here are just a few:

1. Profits are at the mercy of the exchange rate.

2. Product modifications required for successful selling overseas may be such that the hoped-for economies of scale may not be achieved.

3. If the product is nearing the end of its life cycle, it may be better to invest resources in new product development rather than trying to export obsolescent products.

Looking at key issues

The two key issues which must be addressed by new exporters:

- **Opportunities** – any decision to trade overseas must be based on the opportunities open to the company abroad. These opportunities *must* be greater than those available in the home market, either:
  (a) because they are in themselves specially attractive in terms of likely profit; or
  (b) because there is a general lack of opportunity in the domestic market.

- **Resources** – the would-be exporter must consider whether it has the managerial, financial and other resources necessary to sell profitably abroad. If not, then a small company would be better advised to limit itself at most to indirect exporting (see Chapter 2). Only when opportunities appear favourable *and* the company has the resources to take advantage of them should the business consider exporting directly, by itself.

UNDERSTANDING MARKET RESEARCH

Market research is simply the systematic gathering, recording, analysis and interpretation of data or problems relating to the market for, and the marketing of, goods and services. There are two types of research – **desk** and **field**. Both are important but desk can usually satisfy most initial requirements.

- **Desk research** involves the location and study of available published data. This is normally referred to as 'secondary research' or 'bibliographical research'.

- **Field research** (primary or original research) involves obtaining information from informants by means of interviews.

Desk research

Desk research can be carried out both here in the UK and abroad, and either should be conducted before doing any field work overseas. What should you try and find out?

- You may start with your own records and company personnel, for it is surprising just how much data or knowledge lies within your own business.

- Obtain competitors' catalogues which provide not only product, but also market information.

- Visit specialist libraries which contain an Aladdin's cave of valuable data. For example, City Business Library, London and the Department of Trade & Industry (DTI) Library in London. Most major cities and towns have central libraries which house international information.

- Consult the Department of Trade and Industry who have 'Country Desks' for either countries, territories or regions of the world. The staff manning these desks are most helpful and can often send you a market report on the country you are aiming to sell to, as well as giving you further specific advice.

- The US Embassy library in London (appointments only) can be particularly useful and foreign embassies too, although they are more interested in their country's exports!

- The United Nations produce statistical data which is not available elsewhere.

- There are numerous indexing and abstracting services and the *Financial Times* regularly features supplements covering countries, markets and industries overseas.

- Check carefully the plethora of 'guides to information sources' which means directories or similar publications which, although offering no market data themselves, act as signposts to other reference works or organisations which could produce the required information. For example:

- government and other official statistics
- trade directories (always a source of real value)
- trade associations (who should know what is going on in their trade nationally or internationally)
- trade and technical journals (a surprising amount can be gleaned from such publications – even the advertisements for personnel recruitment).

● Always try and short circuit the work cycle by checking to see if market survey reports on your product/market have been previously published. There is no point in re-inventing the wheel!

● Chambers of commerce are usually anxious to help exporters and can provide market intelligence for many parts of the world. You may be asked to join the local chamber!

● The major banks have international divisions which are able to provide useful information, particularly relating to finance, tax and economic trends.

● Major accounting firms with international clients regularly publish data which can be referred to in libraries but often these tend to specialise in certain aspects of overseas business. However, they can help form a good background to your desk research.

Doing desk research abroad
If you are doing desk research abroad yourself or getting someone local to do it on your behalf, then you or they will probably follow much the same work pattern. A word of caution, however!

● Data on specific products or product groups which you might expect to be available in the UK will often not be produced – particularly in developing countries.

● Information, if available, may be years out of date – so check when it was produced, by whom and for whom.

● The data may be of suspect reliability, especially if it was based on some purely tax-based function such as VAT.

- It may prove to be impossible to compare data from one country with another, despite all the continuing efforts to standardise methods and formats.

It is advisable also to check:

- what products were included in the classification
- who collected the data and why, and whether there was any motive for misrepresentation
- how reliable were the methods of data collection.

Remember that this country has probably one of the most accurate and up-to-date systems of collecting, recording and presenting data anywhere in the world but that not all countries invest the same care and attention that we do.

Field research
The problems with field research carried out overseas stem basically from the linguistic, social, cultural and environmental differences between nations.

Setting aside the cost element, your organisation must decide what extra benefits will emerge from conducting field research over and above what can be gained from purely desk research. In case you dismiss field research as an irrelevance, many a large company has failed or not succeeded as well or as quickly as it might through failure to get to grips with actualities in the chosen markets.

The methods of doing field research overseas do not vary from those used in this country but there are some points to watch out for:

- *Sampling*. In many developing countries you will not be able to draw a reliable probability sample, usually because demographic statistics are either out of date or non-existent.

Example
Sampling in India is taken very seriously and uses sophisticated systems. However, commercial research covers only the top sections of the population and devious devices are used to locate them. One consumer study covering durables was based solely on a random selection of private telephone numbers.

- *Questionnaires*. Every questionnaire requires the most careful preparation if it is to produce the amount and accuracy of the information looked for.

- *Telephone interviewing.* This is fine for countries where telephone penetration is high but where it is low, then even for industrial research, this method will not feature as an alternative.

- *Personal interviews.* Again this system is fine in well-developed countries and it is heavily favoured. Personal interviewing becomes even more important in countries where reliable printed data is not available. This, however, poses additional problems in that the recruitment of suitable people is difficult, refusal rates are high due to local cultures, mistrust or suspicion, or plain refusal to divulge any information regarding business to any outside sources.

Using DIY or agency research
There are benefits and downsides for using either.

Doing DIY research abroad
There are times when doing DIY research abroad is appropriate:

- where the research is industrial and only requires a limited number of interviews

- where the organisation has a great deal of specialist knowledge or wants to acquire that knowledge in a certain market

- where the business has appropriate skills to do the work

- where no competent or available agency exists.

Using agency research abroad
Sometimes it is advisable to employ an agency to do the research:

- where the exporter has little or no experience of the market

- where a clear need for an independent and objective assessment is necessary *eg* a potential joint venture

- where the research is highly specialised *eg* motivation research.

Companies new to exporting may not need to carry out any field work overseas but it is surprising how much valuable data can be gathered even on a short visit if you know who to speak to and how to evaluate the responses.

Case study
A manufacturer of standby power generators researched the market in a
major European country. The results 'proved' that a superb market exist-
ed. Checks made locally in various regions showed on the other hand,
that because of the way the power supplies were organised and backed
up, there was little, if any, need for the company's products. An expensive export 'programme' was avoided. Mere figures alone did not give
the proper picture.

Examining selective markets
Two approaches to the location of suitable countries or market segments
within countries are open to exporters:

- Define carefully the characteristics of the foreign consumers most
  likely to buy the firm's products and then examine countries in
  order see later, page 25.

- Determine the countries or markets in which it will be the easiest to
  sell your product – for example, language compatibility or business
  systems and methods are alike and then adapt the output and
  promotion to fit the market.

  Some points for new exporters to consider:

- *Market size*: the bigger a country's population, the better (usually),
  as there is a better chance for more prospects to be addressed.

- *Population structure*: age, sex, density. For example, Singapore
  with a population of 'only' 3 million has a very high proportion of
  under 30-year-olds compared to the overall numbers. This will
  influence what is bought.

- *Storage and distribution facilities*: beware of climatic problems –
  from Arctic cold to equatorially hot – for components, storage time,
  shelf-life and methods of transport. Exporters must take account of
  security in transit and storage, breakages and safety, and plan
  accordingly.

- *Local competition*: do not discount local competition who may control
  distribution channels and have easy access to local capital markets.

Note:
Competitive intensity is more important the simpler the product and
hence the greater the difficulty of brand differentiation.

Categorising prospect markets

- list the criteria to be used in a market's analysis:
  - tariff levels
  - transport costs
  - size of market
  - ease of promotion (advertising restrictions)
  - competition
  - risk factors (payment, government, legal *etc*)
  - distribution.

- give 'weights' to the perceived importance of each variable

- all countries/markets that offer profit potential are then listed

- candidate countries are then more fully researched under the selected criteria

- group the countries into three sectors:
  - possibles
  - probables
  - no-hopers

- discard the no-hopers immediately

- intensify the research on the possibles and, if appropriate, promote them to the probably category

- allocate points to each variable for each remaining country

- if essential, take outside advice.

Advice
Do not attempt to sell or break into too many markets at once. You will have insufficient resources, knowledge or experience. Better by far is to concentrate on a small, select number of countries, possibly nearer to the UK – and build from there.

Finding help for market research
Overseas Trade Services – a unit of the Department of Trade and Industry

and the FCO (Foreign and Commonwealth Office) has a staff of more than 2,000 dedicated to helping UK exporters.

Here is a résumé of what can be made available.

- **Specialist market knowledge.** The branch supplies information and advice on individual markets and regions, updates on legislation and regulations plus opportunities for trade.

- **Research – Export Market Information Centre (EMIC).** This centre, based in London, provides access to a self-help information facility to research potential markets with on-line databases and CD-ROMS.

- **Export Intelligence Service.** This service is provided by PRE-LINK Limited who collect information daily from sources worldwide on new opportunities for UK firms to do business overseas (company subscription service only).

- **Market Information Enquiry Service (MIES).** When you have identified the market to be more fully investigated, the MIES can establish the prospects for specific products/services. The MIES is a charged service from £35–£355 depending on the time factor.

- **Export Marketing Research Scheme (EMRS).** This scheme is administered by the Association of British Chambers of Commerce for the DTI and is designed to help companies use market and marketing research – collection, collating, evaluation and presentation of data – on which export marketing decisions can be based. Funds are available to companies with fewer than 200 employees (but not for research in the EU). Details are available from the Association of British Chambers of Commerce. Also available is advice on how to set about export market research. This scheme is well worth investigating as up to half the cost of commissioning professional consultants to undertake research can be covered if all the criteria can be met.

Advice

While research is undoubtedly necessary for a small or new exporter seeking to expand his business, the aim should be to try to keep it to *essentials* because it does cost (even with grants or aid) and no direct revenue results from it. Sometimes the findings produce an unhelpful or conflicting answer.

Two alternatives to research are

- test marketing

- trade missions.

Test marketing
Test marketing is merely selling in one or more parts of the world and using the experience gained to show you what you are doing right or where you are going wrong.

To make the 'test' really effective, you should choose areas or schemes which are as comparable as possible so that you can determine, fairly, which produces the 'best' results (whatever your criteria are).

Example
Sell to Belgium to see how things might go in the rest of Europe (it is close to home) or, if you want to sell into North America, select an area south of Toronto around Windsor and then expand south into the USA around Chicago. It is said that if you can sell there, you can sell anywhere in the USA!

Test marketing does require more finesse than this, of course, but it does have the merit of being a quick and cheap way of finding out what is possible.

Trade missions
Clearly the best way to carry out research into prospective markets is to visit, but for small companies this can be expensive. One way to avoid such cost is to go on a **DTI outward mission**. These are arranged by a trade association, chamber of commerce or any approved non-profit-making body (not available for Europe or North America).

Advantages of trade missions
Missions are arranged by people who know contacts, systems, opportunities and allow the exporter to concentrate on negotiating and fact-finding. A proportion of the costs are met by the DTI which means that such missions become most attractive to smaller businesses trying to break into exporting.

MODIFYING YOUR PRODUCT

A new exporter would be well-advised to try to sell its output without having to modify or amend it in any way.

Standardisation is ideal as it means:

● *Production economies of scale* – *eg* Coca Cola sells exactly the same product in every country it operates in. However, not every product will be so lucky. For example, Campbell tried to sell its US tomato soup formulation here in the UK, only to discover that the taste was unacceptable to the British palate.

● *Development costs* – a standardised product allows amortisation costs over a larger turnover:
  – stock costs are kept lower
  – fewer components
  – consumer mobility – for travellers and tourists who use, say, Kodak film, Nestlé baby food, Hilton hotels *etc.*
  – some markets take products without any change – *eg* the youth market for jeans, discs.

Some changes may have to be made because of:

● consumer tastes (*eg* foodstuffs)
● low purchasing power which may mean a lowering of quality
● low technical skills overseas meaning product simplification
● poor or low maintenance standards overseas – which could again lead to either improvements in product reliability (no bad thing!) or product simplification (again, a good thing!).

The following is a list of changes which may be *forced* upon you:

● *legal requirements* – special product standards

● *tariffs*

● *nationalism* – some countries may demand that a percentage of components should be locally made

● *technical* – *eg* measuring, calibration, voltage

● *taxation* – *eg* car tax related to engine size or, as in Singapore, car rationing by financial measures

● *climate* – as mentioned earlier, depending on climate, some products may need to be amended. Example: car tyre composition varies according to the extremes of climate.

Packaging, labelling and servicing

As is the case with the actual product, packaging is subject to pressures tending towards standardisation on the one hand and, on the other, towards adaptation to special market needs.

In arriving at the correct decision, both the protectional and promotional aspects of packaging should be considered.

Protection
When deciding whether to change the packaging of your product consider:

- climatic conditions in the market-place and in transit
- the handling the product is going to receive
- the time the product is in the distribution chain
- customer usage rate and consequent storage time.

Promotion
The packaging may also have to change in order to promote your product overseas. Consider the following factors.

- *Package size* – as already mentioned, in poorer countries items such as razor blades, chewing gum and cigarettes may be sold individually.

- *Packaging cost* – is the standard package over-elaborate for overseas?

- *Packaging colours* – eg white is associated with death or mourning in the Far East.

- *Legal requirements* – for example, some countries do not allow on-pack promotional gifts (Venezuela) and countries in the EU now have very strict requirements as to what must be shown on pack (see labelling).

● *Literacy* – low levels of literacy may require more graphic illustration than existing copy on packs/packaging.

The construction of the pack should therefore take into account a number of important factors which will also include recyclability (stiff laws in the EU) and re-use of packaging materials for other purposes. There is one most important condition which applies to consignment going to Australia which prevents untreated timber being used for crating cargo as this could lead to severe problems on that continent.

Getting advice
Although new exporters may be concerned about all the many aspects of getting their product, packaging and promotion right, the reality is, that by making a number of enquiries with expert or well-informed bodies you can avoid serious and costly errors. Regarding the actual arrangements for consigning an order which involves crating or special packaging, it is best to consult a forwarding agent who will have specialist knowledge about sending shipments to various parts of the world including how to pack them for security *etc* (see Chapter 5 on freight forwarding).

Labelling and government regulations
Exporters must adhere to labelling regulations in every country. These, of course, vary widely but usually they require an indication of the *manufacturer, country of origin* (extremely important), *weight* (usually metric but not in the USA where imperial measurements are still used), *description of the contents, nature of the ingredients.* There may well be other specific additional information required but details of these can be obtained from the Overseas Tariffs and Regulations Section of the Department of Trade and Industry.

Language
Whatever government regulations say about the contents of the label on a product, the manufacturer must have a label which will communicate information to customers which will help make it easier for them to use the product, help in providing consumer satisfaction and to encourage trial and repeat purchase.

Make sure that the label is written in the appropriate language(s) throughout except where some national image is supremely important such as French perfume and Scotch whisky. What exporters can do to avoid excessive costs is to use multilingual labels covering several countries but this will only really work well if a multinational image will make a good impression. Otherwise you will have to incur the extra costs to ensure an entirely national image.

Perversely, many products sold into former USSR or Comecon (economic association of communist countries) countries only sell well with English labels (not Russian or whichever language) as English is perceived to invest a special status on the product or garment – one which means that the owner can afford to buy a better-quality product!

Servicing
One of the reasons that Japanese cars succeeded so well when they were first launched into the UK was not only that they were more reliable, but also because they were so well backed up with service. Indeed, the Japanese used a great number of resources in getting everything in place before a single car was sold. For those goods, such as cars, which require these facilities, customers will give preference to national products if they have the slightest reason to worry about after-sales service from a far-off foreign country. A *clear, international, servicing policy* is therefore a must.

There are basically two principal ways of providing after-sales service.

1. **Distributors**: Ideally an exporter would appoint a reliable distributor who already has an organised servicing network compatible with the product. Sadly, such distributors are rare, so involvement by the original manufacturer/exporter in the service function becomes inescapable. Exporters may have to train personnel at their own company headquarters, have a team of travelling trainers, or even second company maintenance or service staff to the distributor.

2. **Direct servicing**: Direct servicing is most usual in the case of heavy or major capital equipment when staff can fly out to effect repairs *etc.*

Concentrating on quality
By concentrating on quality and small quantities, new or small exporters reduce the service problem to minor proportions. Orders should be sent, where appropriate, with spare parts as part of the deal.

If there is a 'returnable' situation, always make sure the system is able to supply a replacement first. If you concentrate on quality and service, then your innovative and entrepreneurial skills should allow you to export almost any kind of goods or services somewhere and to keep customers coming back for more.

Case study
In Africa a hand-operated crop duster made by an American company was widely used by cotton farmers. Although it did turn easily, it needed a great deal of maintenance. In a relatively short while the gears 'froze up' and broke because it required so much servicing. As a result, the government, who had loaned the American machine to farmers, went back to a heavier, old, poorer-performing, French machine which lasted longer and required less servicing.

UNDERSTANDING TRADE MARKS AND BRAND NAMES

What is a **trade mark**? Why is it important? What is a **brand**? How can you protect them?

● **Trade mark**: A trade mark is a brand or part of a brand that is given legal protection because it is capable of exclusive appropriation (*ie* it belongs to the originator).

● **Brand**: A brand is a name, term, sign, symbol or design, shape, smell or combination of them, which is intended to identify the goods or services of one seller or group of sellers and to differentiate them from competitors.

Knowing why a trade mark is important

A trade mark identifies the origin of the product. It is also the purchaser's assurance of quality, as well as allowing the manufacturer to promote his own product without benefiting his rivals.

A trade mark's protection – by registration – is often vital. Sometimes it can be the difference between success or failure for the business.

Although protection is seldom easy, it becomes even more difficult internationally, partly because of the problems connected with registration (which should at least now be much simpler in the European Union (EU) because of a central registration point), but also because of brand imitation and brand piracy in many countries.

Seek the advice of an agent who specialises in trade marks, brand names and also patents. The cost should be treated as insurance, as should the costs for international trade mark protection.

Beware of trade mark imitation which aims to take advantage of the reputation and promotional expenditure of a supplier by making similar products under the same, or very similar name as the original, complete with packaging and labelling.

Beware also of trade mark piracy which is the registration of brand names with the aim of selling them back to the companies which originated them, if and when such firms wish to enter the market.

Consider the present and likely future market potential:

● ease and cost of registering

● the expense and inconvenience of having to select another brand name if it becomes necessary

● how valuable or important the brand name is – in industrial goods it is usually not so vital

● whether it is important to establish one standard international brand name – for films (Kodak), or Scotch whisky (*eg* Johnny Walker), it is vital.

Any infringement of trade mark law when discovered or reported should be tackled immediately through the courts. The Institute of Trade Mark Agents (see Useful Contacts) will advise on both national and international registration.

Choosing your brand name

It is wise to find an international name that has no actual meaning in any other language. By using a made-up word or set of numbers you will avoid the trap that some exporters have fallen into, as illustrated by the following case studies.

Case studies

Ford Motor Company launched a low-cost truck, the 'Fiera', into some less-developed countries. Sadly, Ford executives failed to check whether Fiera had any meaning in another language. In Spanish it means 'ugly old woman'. Sales suffered in Spanish-speaking countries. Also in the motor world Ford launched a pricey car into Mexico under the name 'Caliente' (was Comet elsewhere). This word is the slang for 'street-walker' and sales, not surprisingly, were correspondingly slow.

Rolls-Royce whose cars sold in Germany under the name 'Silver Mist' soon realised why the model should have its name changed when it was pointed out that 'mist' in German meant 'excrement'.

Kodak was selected by a panel who wanted a word that had no meaning but was easily pronounceable by everyone, and Exxon (Esso when pronounced phonetically means 'stalled car' in Japan) was also deliberately constructed to avoid gaffes and to be internationally safe on all counts!

DECIDING WHICH PARTS OF THE WORLD TO EXPORT TO

Europe (the European Union)
Around half of our exports go to mainland Europe – countries within the European Union. What can be made and sold in this country can usually be sold without problems other than labelling changes in these countries.

Payment for your overseas sales in the EU should not present too many worries, although you should never ease up on credit status checking or control on any customer. Some caution should be exercised when initially extending credit. Eastern Europe still poses a number of concerns and is not yet totally settled politically or economically.

A number of UK organisations have entered into joint venture arrangements since this appears to make it quicker and easier to break into or set up in these markets. With local know-how such an arrangement would make sense. But for the smaller exporter ensuring payment in full and on time may be the biggest worry of all.

Many former Communist-controlled countries are still coming to terms with or trying to understand Western styles of business, commerce and trade which handicaps their international development. However, as many of these countries are seeking admission to the EU, the long-term prospects for them would seem to be promising.

The Middle East
The Middle East is a very wealthy region, where Britain has historically traded well. There have been, and will probably continue to be periods of unrest but British quality goods have always been well received in this region.

The Far East
This region has been regarded for many years as the fastest-growing economy with massive increases in productivity *etc* being posted by a whole list of countries from Japan, Singapore, Hong Kong, Thailand, Malaysia, Philippines, Indonesia and Australia/New Zealand. Now China is regarded as the new powerhouse of this thriving region. Some say the rate of growth has declined but, again, this could be a momentary pause for there is a huge and pent-up demand for class British goods which are presented and promoted in the best possible fashion. This covers both consumer and capital projects where British firms have been consistently successful over many years.

India
India is one of the world's top 10 industrial nations, and with a

population of around 800mn, represents a huge market, one in which approximately 200mn are classified as middle class with the yen for good-class Western-style products.

Now that the country has begun its liberalisation programme, opportunities for progressive exporters are rapidly increasing, but it is wise to work with or through agents or distributors who know the ropes.

South Africa

Having 're-invented' itself with the election of President Mandela, South Africa is undergoing a number of problems – educational, economic, financial *etc*. However, the advice from the DTI, which is spending half its promotional budget on getting British exporters to sell in South Africa, is to get into this vibrant and exciting market before our competitors – Germany, France, Italy, Japan and the USA – clean up before we have even left the starting blocks. If you trade there, advice is to take out credit risk insurance if you are not using letters of credit, and monitor payments very tightly.

Central Africa

Since the UK, in relation to other parts of the world, has very little trade with Central Africa, the only advice to those who are even thinking about it is to *think again*. This is one of the world's trickiest trade areas.

North Africa

There are parts of North Africa which, like Libya, are out of bounds for much of what Britain exports. Other North African countries such as Morocco and Egypt are now much more stable and represent good trading opportunities.

North America

The whole of North America makes up the world's wealthiest and largest trading block and is also the most fiercely competitive. If you plan to sell into the USA, do it via Canada and then only take in a part of the States initially – the country is so large that you may find you have to adapt some aspect of your marketing arrangements.

The USA has no real *need* to import anything, so if you are hoping to get your product into the USA, you must be able to prove why it excels over locally or nationally produced goods – and then deliver every time.

Caribbean

The Caribbean is an underestimated but useful area for British goods to be sold into. There is a great deal of development underway which should improve the purchasing abilities of the Caribbean countries – even Cuba.

Remember, though, that English is not the only language spoken – French, Spanish and Dutch are also spoken. Make sure also your products are in tune with local customs and culture.

South America
Whereas trade with many South American countries was either not done or fraught with problems (fraud, currency, transport, distribution, duties/customs *etc*), nowadays many countries have made big efforts to put these 'difficulties' behind them. Chile for one can be held up as an example even to Western standards, showing its neighbours what determination and good government can do.

A few points to remember
In all the areas of the globe where it is 'safe' to trade there are just a few basic points to bear in mind.

● Will what I make sell there?
● How do I sell it there?
● How and when will I be paid?

The DTI country desk (see Useful Contacts) for each country will be able to advise you on a number of points but there is no short cut to finding out for yourself the full implications of selling goods somewhere you know very little about. Wherever you trade, first do your homework, following any advice, and use the information contained in this book.

2
Organising Your Selling Overseas

DISTINGUISHING BETWEEN CUSTOMERS, CONSUMERS AND USERS

For the sake of clarity, you should try to distinguish between **customers, consumers** and **users** because the terms are frequently used with little clear indication of what is meant by them. 'Customer' in export is best used for a person or company who orders from you, to whom you deliver the goods and who pays you for them.

Sometimes customers will be users. For example a textile manufacturer in India will perhaps purchase new machinery for his factory. Therefore, he will be both a customer and user. On the other hand, an Italian importer of cotton yarn may not use it to make cloth but resell it to textile manufacturers to use, in which case if you were the exporter of the yarn you would be dealing with a customer who would not be the user. In many cases therefore, you will actually be selling to customers who are *users* or to customers who are *reselling* to users.

With consumer goods (including durables) it is unlikely that the importer (your customer) will be the end user or consumer. The importer will be reselling to others who will sell finally to the consumer or final user.

These consumers can therefore be a long way from the original importer. If you sell services then you will probably use the term 'client'. If you sell skills then your clients/buyers will be licensees, franchise holders or franchisees.

Understanding why this distinction is important
The reason why this distinction is important is that as a new exporter you must decide to whom you will physically sell your goods. Next you must decide which distribution channels, if any, they will pass through on their way to the final user or consumer. Selecting the correct distribution channel will therefore tell you where you should be directing your selling efforts.

There are two functions:

● *distribution* overseas
● *selling* overseas.

This chapter sets out to show you how to organise the function of who you sell to.

DETERMINING THE GROUPS OF USERS AND CUSTOMERS

It is probably a good idea to consider first the users or consumers because they will more often than not determine the type of customer to whom you should export – from whom the users and consumers will draw their supplies.

Example
You sell ceramic tiles. You will probably have two types of users – industrial (for factories and commercial properties) and households who buy for decorative reasons.

You will probably sell direct to the industrial user (or via an agent/distributor – whose roles are discussed later in the chapter) but probably to a wholesale organisation for the retail trade.

If you sell speciality foods, then your sales outlets will not be the normal food outlets but from stores specialising in 'unusual' foods. Your customers will therefore have to use different channels of distribution.

It is useful to try to build up a profile of your overseas customers.

Case study
A small engineering company making and selling temperature control equipment for factories found that in Germany three things were demanded:

1. The products had to conform to every German technical specification; had, of course, to be totally reliable; replacement parts had to be available – plus service – in Germany. Price was not a serious factor.

2. German customers wanted to buy from a British company direct (not via a distributor) with all details quoted in German and prices DDP (Delivered Duty Paid) in DMs.

3. The German customer wanted a German technical representative to call on them but he had to be local to their own region!

The UK supplier appointed several commission agents who handled some two-thirds of all imports with Germany.

Note:

The Germans preferred not to be swayed by any direct mail (never read it) or advertising. There were already a number of German competitors but customers were willing to switch to the UK *provided* they were convinced of the suppliers' commitment to selling to Germany – which included selling or showing at trade shows *etc* in Germany.

It took longer to sell into Germany than was first anticipated but the results have been worthwhile.

In France, however, a totally different view of the buying process applied and the UK exporter had to sell to customers whose needs were different and who also acted in a different (Gallic!) way to the Germans.

EXPLORING OTHER EXPORT OPPORTUNITIES

Selling directly

As we have seen, some products need to be sold to the user. In other cases sales will be made to governments and in some countries major wholesalers will only buy direct from the supplier. Selling directly this way naturally has many advantages in that the process avoids 'middlemen' and direct negotiation can be established between the two parties. However useful this direct approach may be and however attractive it may sound, you may feel that it is somewhat beyond your company's capabilities to become involved with consumers and users overseas. Additionally, you may not want to deal even with those customers abroad who supply them.

What this then means is that you have the choice of leaving the actual exporting in the hands of others so far as this is possible, or you may feel that a compromise is best, whereby you deal with a limited number of overseas territories, leaving the rest to others.

So, if you decide to limit your dealings to customers in Britain, there are several export opportunities you can exploit, without setting foot outside the country. These include:

- manufacturers
- export houses
- confirming houses
- buying or indent houses
- export concessionaires
- specialist export managers

- Crown Agents
- international trading companies
- UK buying offices
- complementary marketing.

Selling to other UK manufacturers

One simple way for new 'exporters' to get their goods overseas is to sell to other **UK manufacturers** and leave them to export. As long as the product meets overseas specifications and other conditions, then you have few worries. A great deal of 'export' trade is conducted this way.

Case study
A bicycle lamp manufacturer sold its production to a bicycle maker who then sold the complete outfit overseas. While this is very much indirect exporting, it does get your product abroad quickly, at low risk and cost.

Using an export house

If you are going to export indirectly you will want to know about the specialist **export houses** and how they can help you.

An export houses is 'any company or firm, not being a manufacturer, whose main activity is the handling or financing of British export trade and/or international trade not connected with the UK'.

There are around 800 export houses in the UK. Between them they handle about 20 per cent of Britain's export trade. There are three major categories:

- *export merchants*, who act as principals in the export transaction; that is, buying and selling on their own account

- *confirming houses* and buying/indent houses, who merely represent the buyer abroad

- *manufacturers' export agents* and specialist export managers who represent the UK manufacturer.

Naturally, some export houses manage to combine a number of the functions mentioned.

What do export merchants do?
Export merchants are no more than domestic wholesalers operating in markets abroad through their own salesmen, agents, stockists and, quite

often, local branch offices. They make their remuneration from the difference between the buying and selling price.

Export merchants tend to specialise in certain territories or in certain ranges of goods.

Assessing the benefits of using a merchant

● The manufacturer can take advantage of the merchant's excellent knowledge of overseas markets, contacts and local systems, which is particularly valuable in difficult markets such as Japan.

● There is no need to finance the export transaction and there is no credit risk.

● Likewise there is no need to become involved in the mechanics of the export process – documentation, shipping or insurance.

● There is no need to invest money or executive time as there is no overhead cost.

● Sometimes 'barter' trade (see Chapter 3) is necessary to do export deals, an area where specialist help is necessary.

● Sometimes a merchant will carry more weight in selling than individual manufacturers or exporters, so it would be sensible to sell through such a merchant who has that type of experience.

The disadvantages of selling through merchants
For all the advantages of selling through a merchant there are a number of drawbacks.

● Probably the most serious drawback is that the exporter has very little or no control over his end market and his products could be dropped by the merchant if a more profitable line comes along.

● No goodwill can be built up by the exporter for his company if he wishes to expand – goodwill only attaches to the export merchant.

● If the merchant is carrying a large number of lines, an exporter's product may receive scant attention or promotion.

● If a merchant does not secure a reasonably quick return, the product may be dropped. Therefore, if any long-term investment of money or time is required to exploit the market, it is unlikely that a merchant will even consider the product in the first place.

Using a confirming house

A **confirming house** confirms as a principal (*ie* a deal in his own right or account) an order which an overseas buyer has placed with the exporter/manufacturer in the UK who is unwilling to extend credit overseas. Therefore the confirming house finances the transaction, accepts the short-term risk and receives a commission for his work from the buyer. So it is little different from trading with a merchant – and the pros and cons are similar.

Using a buying or indent house

The **buying house** acts purely on behalf of the overseas buyer, either buying with an open brief against orders received, or placing indents on manufacturers whom the buyer has specified.

Sometimes the buying house may act as a principal, very much in the same way as a confirming house. Advantages, or disadvantages, to the exporter are basically the same as for a merchant house.

Using export concessionaires or export agents

If you decide you have no wish to work with any of these organisations, you may decide to use the services of an **export concessionaire**, who will either buy from you and resell on his own account or he will obtain orders for you to execute and then attend to all the export paperwork for you. As the exporter, you pay an agreed rate for commission.

Concessionaires operate either on a worldwide scale, or specialise in specific areas where they have good connections.

Assessing the benefits of using an export concessionaire
These are basically similar to those of trading through an export merchant except:

● export finance, credit risk, shipping insurance and export documents remain the responsibility of the exporter/manufacturer

● the manufacturer retains greater control over his market than via the other methods of exporting.

Using a specialist export manager

The **specialist export manager** offers a complete export management service, in effect becoming the export department of the manufacturer. He will act in the manufacturer's name, even using the manufacturer's own letterheading.

Normally an export manager will undertake finance and documentation and perhaps assume credit risk. The export manager is paid by commission on sales but often an annual retainer is paid as well.

If such a person sounds ideal for you, take a look at the disadvantages as well as the benefits before leaping in and retaining one.

Advantages

● You 'gain' an immediate export department at low overhead cost.

● You secure and keep the greatest control over the markets you/he is selling into.

● You therefore build up your own goodwill in these markets.

● You can keep a long-term relationship if you believe that is the way you wish to continue.

Disadvantages

● The manager is subjected to the same pressures as any other indirect merchant house and will drop or not promote slow or unprofitable lines.

● If sales grow, then the manufacturer should consider exporting on his own account or directly but will not have gained sufficient experience to go it alone.

● The problem with specialist managers is that they will want a worldwide brief but will not be able to offer worldwide coverage.

Advice
Make sure that the markets you have targeted coincide with the specialist's genuine contacts and experience.

Using the Crown Agents
Exporters should be aware of the **Crown Agents**, which is a public

service working for principals in the public sectors overseas, for example governments, transport authorities, power organisations, military, universities and schools in around 50 countries.

The Crown Agents buy anything from power stations to banknotes and stamps. What will please exporters is that they pay suppliers in the UK, so are customers with whom you can happily trade.

Such trade will allow you to export 'travel free', as it were, and while it may seem like exporting second-hand (just like selling through export merchants), it may well be another simple answer to your export problems, especially for smaller companies in the initial stages of their exporting career.

Working with international trading companies

International trading companies are highly diversified and large-scale manufacturers and merchants, operating often at both wholesale and retail levels of distribution.

In South-East Asia and in the former African colonial territories they are particularly useful. For a British exporter it is somewhat akin to trading with a UK merchant house. Because of their size and coverage they are attractive to exporters as distributors.

Example
UAC International, with its headquarters in London, is one of the largest trading organisations in Africa. Made up of 300 or so companies, who often compete with one another, it trades in most tropical African states. Not only does it have manufacturing interests, but also wholesaling and distribution activities covering both industrial and consumer goods. It also has its own shipping fleet and runs a chain of department stores. Such an organisation could be most useful to small exporters.

Using UK buying offices

Many of the major department stores in developed countries maintain buying offices here in the UK and others appoint a UK export house as their buying agent.

Example
All Japan's top department stores have buying offices or representatives in London. Top German stores Karstadt AG and Hertie GmbH have their own buying offices in London. Between them these two groups control over 250 department or chain store outlets – accounting for upwards of 7 per cent of all retail turnover in Germany. It is worthwhile getting to know the various buyers who, between them, wield considerable clout.

If overseas stores do not have an agent or office here, buyers will visit the UK on a regular basis, and their arrival is often published in either trade journals or through the DTI's Intelligence Service.

Understanding complementary marketing

Complementary marketing otherwise known as 'piggy-back' exporting works like this:

- A manufacturer (the *carrier*) uses his established overseas distribution network to market another manufacturer's goods (the *rider*) alongside his own. Two alternative systems could apply:

  - the carrier sells the rider's products on a commission basis – becoming in effect an agent; or
  - the carrier buys the products outright and sells them at the best price he can get – acting then as a merchant.

Assessing the advantages for the rider
Complementary exporting provides a simple and low-risk method of beginning export activities, which is so important for new or small companies who perhaps lack the resources to export directly.

Assessing the advantages for the carrier
Very simply, the carrier can broaden his own perhaps limited range, offering economies of scale in distribution and filling downturns in seasonal items.

Additionally, a rider's product may help the sales of the carrier's own lines.

Example
A well-known sewing machine company piggy-backs products closely associated with its own – *eg* fabrics, patterns, threads and accessories.

Advice
Piggy-back arrangements need to be entered into carefully and the reasons why a 'carrier' wants to take on a 'rider' should be studied carefully. Additionally, piggy-back arrangements are inevitably subject to strain but they do work well for some.

What is perhaps a more suitable method of working with others is an export consortium. This is a group of companies who agree to form a unit to bid for a major project – *eg* the construction industry – because singly they would never be able to mount a bid. Care must be taken however, to ensure the stability of all the partners and how the legalities and finances are to be set up and controlled.

Direct sales

There are naturally many instances when it will not only be possible but essential to make sales/exports **direct** to the user/consumer without the need for a middle man at all. Here are some examples:

- industrial goods
- goods sold to national governments, local authorities and other official bodies
- consumer goods sold by direct mail
- consumer goods sold to retail stores, where they are large enough
- goods sold to mail order houses (not to be confused with direct mail which is an entirely different method of selling).

A few words about mail order houses. These tend to be extremely demanding as delivery must be 100 per cent guaranteed, and prices must remain unchanged for the period of the validity of the catalogue. This could also lead to problems with the exchange rate.

Watch out also for the mail order houses who often want an 'exclusive' – which means you cannot offer that product to another outlet or competitor. This could severely limit the value of such an outlet in any one country. However, it could lead to other exciting opportunities if the one particular line sells well, but you will have to weigh the pros and cons extremely carefully before you make such a lengthy commitment.

UNDERSTANDING AGENTS AND HOW THEY WORK

Having discussed the various direct and indirect methods of selling and marketing your exports, we must now look to the rôles of the agent and distributor who may be selling on your behalf in overseas territories.

Agency may be defined as the legal relationship which exists when one person or company (**agent**) is 'employed' by another person or company (**principal**) to bring to that principal (or you as the exporter) a contractual relationship with third parties. A sales agent is therefore employed to bring about a **sales contract** between his principal and a third party – the customer.

Note: The term 'employed' is not used to describe the agent as a paid or salaried employee, as the agent works on a commission basis of one sort or another.

The legal title to the goods being exported never actually passes to the agent. It passes from the exporter (principal) direct to the customer, the agent receiving a commission by way of remuneration. There are four main types of agent and it is important for the new exporter to know what each does or is responsible for.

1. Commission agent

The **commission agent** sells with the aid of samples and/or catalogues. He does not (or should not) hold any stock. An agent merely passes orders to his principal – you, the exporter, who in turn effects delivery and collects the money or payment.

This type of agency is particularly suited to industrial goods.

2. Stocking agent

This type of agent, as the title suggests, does stock the product. In addition, he will provide storage and handling facilities. However, he still does not take title to the goods.

This type of agent expects not only his commission but also a fixed sum to cover storage and handling.

3. Agency with spares and servicing facilities

Similarly an agency may carry spares, parts and provide repair services for which he will charge the customer at a scale of charges agreed with the principal (you, the exporter).

4. Del credere agent

The fourth type of agent is not so much an agent but more of a contractual arrangement which could apply to any agency agreement. In selling through an agent, you will not get to know the customer as well as your agent, especially when it comes to credit rating, even if you have done a search on some of the more important of them through a credit search/rating company here or in the country to which you are exporting.

The **del credere agent** takes on the credit risk and agrees to pay you, his principal, if the customer defaults. Such an agent may well ask you for a higher rate of commission to compensate for this extra risk. In territories which you are not familiar with, a del credere agent could be less expensive than taking out credit risk insurance (see Chapter 7).

Deciding which type of agent to use
Check out carefully which type of agent will fit the bill for your product or activity and then do your sums accordingly.

Agencies vary, in size as well as in make up. They may be individuals, partnerships or small companies specialising in representation. They may also be large-scale merchants or trading houses as we have described earlier – or even major manufacturers using the rider/carrier piggy-back method of agency representation.

Appointing an agent

Advantages
Agents are relied upon in export because they offer a number of advantages.

● The exporter has the services of an experienced local national who will know the local business practices as well as your industry.

● Hopefully the agent's existing product lines and contacts will make it easier to introduce your products into the local market.

● You, as the exporter, gain quick experience of the market and you can test the potential of the market.

● Your investment cost is virtually nil.

● Results (if all goes well) will be instant.

Disadvantages
There are also some disadvantages to appointing an agent.

● Many companies are blinded by the quick success promised by an agent or they fail to study the disadvantages which follow in the wake of the hastily appointed agent.

● If an agent is handling a number of lines, he cannot be expected to give all his attention to yours.

● Agents cannot afford to take a long-term view of the market, so if sales are not quickly forthcoming, he may well be tempted to ignore it in favour of others.

● A serious problem for you as the exporter arises when the market potential is beyond the resources of the agent to fully develop. You are then stuck with an appointed agent who cannot cope.

● Once sales begin to take off, it will become less expensive and more efficient to open your own branch office than to keep paying the agent's commission.

Clearly there are not, and cannot be, any rules as to when an agency is the correct method by which to export and sell. For new exporters the following may help.

● An agency is only one channel among the various ones considered earlier.

● An agency alternative should be compared with these alternatives in the light of the criteria set out earlier.

● The appointment of an agent requires careful planning, selection, motivation/payment and supervision. These aspects are discussed on pages 52–57, along with the legal implications now affecting the role, duties and functions of both agents and principal in the EU.

UNDERSTANDING DISTRIBUTORS AND HOW THEY WORK

Distributors often get classified as agents, but they carry out a totally different function. A **distributor** is defined as a customer who has been granted exclusive or preferential rights to **purchase and resell** a range of products or services in specified areas or markets.

Basically then, a distributor is a wholesaler whose remuneration comes from the difference between the purchase price (from the exporter) and the selling price (to the consumer/user or retailer). *No commission is paid to a distributor.*

However, a distributor differs from a normal wholesaler by virtue of the 'exclusive or preferential rights' granted him. A distributor's relationship with his supplier is one of principal and principal, not one of agent and principal.

There are four main types of distributor and it is essential that, if an exporter appoints a distributor, he should understand how each one operates and therefore which type should be appointed.

1. Sole distributor
Where a **sole distributor** is appointed, no other distributor will be appointed in that territory. You, as the manufacturer or exporter however, can, exercise your right to sell in that territory.

2. Exclusive distributor
Here even the manufacturer/exporter is debarred – unless the agreement permits otherwise – from selling the contracted goods (note the word *contracted* as this then refers specifically to a product, range or group).

Nor can you appoint another distributor in that territory.

3. Non-exclusive distributor

A manufacturer/exporter in this case would be permitted to sell directly into the territory *and* also appoint other distributors in the territory.

4. Selective distributor

This type of system could be appropriate where the goods include technical equipment which a manufacturer/exporter feels should only be supplied to approved dealers.

Example

A dealer may have to employ staff with particular skills – *eg* scientific, electronic, computer, photographic, engineering or construction *etc* and, if they cannot meet these criteria (now or at a future set date), they will be refused entry into the distribution system.

Other distributors may have to have not only skilled staff, but also specialist equipment in order to satisfactorily sell and service the product. A car distributor will obviously need a sales forecourt and workshops.

What are stockists?

Stockists are distributors who receive a special price, discount, purchase terms or credit terms in return for undertaking to hold specified minimum levels of stock of a specified range of products.

Example

Furniture stores are often appointed stockists; the appointment of a stockist is usually made when big ticket items are being sold – either durable or semi-durable (*eg* clothes).

Note

The granting of exclusivity or preferential terms usually implies the formal appointment of a distributor and the preparation of a distributorship agreement.

Case study

An international medical/therapeutic manufacturing company, whose regional European offices were in London, appointed a French distributor with the exclusive rights to the whole of France, which meant that even the manufacturer/supplier was debarred from selling in that country.

All went well for the first year with the distributor, based in Paris, producing good results, helped by the training received from the supplier.

After the first year, matters began to go wrong, sales began to drop, advertising failed to produce enough good enquiries and more than a few questions were asked by the supplier. After a further six months the supplier sent over to Paris its own UK sales manager on long-term loan to try and sort out the problem.

Instead of turning round the business, it went further downhill and the question of personalities began to assume a major importance. The French distributor, feeling that his business was being usurped, told the London office that he wanted to have the sales manager returned to the UK and that he wanted to run things his own way. The UK office, who had appointed the distributor, said that unless he agreed to a number of fresh proposals, the distributorship would be taken away. There was now acrimony on both sides.

The French distributor went to court in Paris and had his case for wrongful termination of contract heard under French law.

The UK company, it transpired, had never actually produced a contract setting out any contractual details and so the distributor quite correctly sued in France.

The case went on for weeks and the distributor won. The costs, apart from legal fees, executive time, travel and hotel charges were exceptionally heavy, with the court awarding damages and other costs to the plaintiff. What was worse though was that the UK office lost a good distributor and a useful contributor to sales and profits.

Advice

Make sure you have a proper contract drawn up to cover the rights and duties of both parties, with provisions or contingencies for situations outlined above. Always make sure you have the right to decide under which country's laws any litigation is to be heard. Just think of what could have been the cost if the case were heard in Moscow or Japan.

Most distributors will expect advice and assistance from you in the marketing of your product and it will be in your best interests if you do provide it.

DECIDING BETWEEN AN AGENT OR A DISTRIBUTOR

How do I know which will be best for me?
Generally, agents can be more closely controlled. They must market the products at the prices and on the terms stipulated by the principal or supplier and you as the exporter/supplier have the right to accept or reject any order generated by the agent.

It is therefore a matter of commercial consideration, rather than a legal issue, which determines whether or not you use an agent or a distributor.

Check

— Is it important for stocks to be held?

— How many customers or stockists are there for the product (too many and it becomes impractical to ship to hundreds of locations)?

— What is the cost of paying compensation to an agent if it does not work out (this applies particularly to agents rather more so than to a distributor)?

Understanding the regulations

Commercial Agents Regulations and EC Directive 86/653
In Europe exporters must be aware of regulations which came into force on 1 January 1994 covering arrangements between principals and their commercial agents.

Key points for exporters to note:

● the method and amount of remuneration, commission and compensation

● exchange certain relevant information

● the notice period of termination and payments which become due

● the scope and duration of restrictive covenants on a commercial agent following termination.

Note
The Directive applies to agents but not to distributors. Individuals, partnerships or companies which buy and sell on their own account for their own profit are not covered either.

RECRUITING, SELECTING AND WORKING WITH AGENTS AND DISTRIBUTORS

Advice
Before working with an agent bear in mind the following two points:

1. Before even thinking about recruiting or finding an agent, you must
    be sure in your own mind, having checked out all the alternatives,
    that an agent is the best person or organisation to sell on your
    behalf.

2. Having decided an agent is what you really need, draw up a **profile**
    of your **own organisation**.

Any competent agent will want to have the fullest possible information about the prospective principal – **you** – so draw up a profile in the
form of a selling document.

The profile should cover not only the usual or obvious subjects such
as product range, numbers of employees, factories, offices *etc* but also:

- your company's recent performance or plans
- the special selling points of your product
- recommended marketing approach
- the help you can or will give to the agent – training, advertising,
  literature *etc*.

With this prepared – it is also good discipline for the company to
have such a profile – you can now begin to approach organisations who
can help you find a suitable agent.

Locating an agent overseas

The most usual sources of information on likely candidates are:

- the Overseas Trade Services' Export Representative Service (ERS)
- Chambers of Commerce
- banks
- trade associations
- agents' associations
- advertising in the appropriate trade journals.

A few words about each will tell you which may be the most useful:

- *Export Representative Service*: This service helps exporters wishing
  to find an overseas representative – agent, distributor or importer –
  for their products. You will receive a report with recommendations
  on potential. Charges for the ERS are time related and range from
  £355–1,065.

- *Chambers of Commerce*: Many Chambers of Commerce make efforts to provide introductions or will pass on enquiries to other Chambers abroad. The London Chamber of Commerce and Industry is excellent in helping with its 'Openings for Trade' (a subscription service).

- *Banks*: Most major banks have an overseas business development service whose role it is to help customers or prospective customers to expand into overseas markets. Indeed, many banks are specially set up to provide introductions between principals and agents.

- *Trade associations*: Many trade bodies have international connections and carry agency opportunities in their newsletters or bulletins. Trade journals are always useful in checking out what is going on in your industry anyway.

- *Agents' associations*: The International Union of Commercial Agents and Brokers (IUCAB) based in Amsterdam covers Western Europe and the USA with a total membership of some 50,000 agents. One of its principal functions is to arrange introductions.

- *Advertising*: There is a huge selection of trade and technical journals to advertise in overseas. Check the international press guides used by advertising agencies for specific details.

Tip
It may be useful to advertise in English in overseas media. This will test the applicants' knowledge of English which may well be important.

Selecting an agent

Visit the market
A company which lacks the financial or management resources to visit markets should ask itself if it should be thinking about exporting or staying in the market.

Procedure

- Talk to all agency executives, sales people, office staff and back-up people.

- Talk to customers who will be buying from the candidate agent.

Then, establish a checklist which should contain some or most of the points described:

- who owns the agency?
- career history of the executives
- what other agencies do they have and what success have they achieved?
- the area to be covered – regularly
- the types of outlet covered
- frequency of calling
- number of sales people/service length
- agency's market knowledge and marketing competence.

● Always get bank and trade references and look for the agency's interest in, and enthusiasm for, what you are offering.

Preparing an agency agreement

When you have found a suitable agent, you must conclude a formal, legal agreement. This should be as short and simple as possible but contain the following essential points:

1. *Parties* to the contract – where they are and their capacity to contract.

2. *Products* – definitions of the products subject to the agreement – now and in the future.

3. *Territory* – a proper definition of the territory in which the agent is entitled to act. For example, does Malaysia include Sarawak and Brunei or just mainland Malaysia?

4. *Exclusivity*

   ● Does the agent have sole/exclusive right to the territory?

   ● Does the exporter have any rights to operate in the agent's territory?

   ● Does the agent have any right to commission on orders placed direct with the supplier/principal?

5. *Rights and duties*

   ● What level of sales and marketing assistance is to be provided, information given to the agent by you the exporter?

● The extent to which the agent must comply with your instructions on prices and conditions of sale.

● Whether any minimum turnover is stipulated.

6. *Commission* – it is vital to get the question of commission straight at the very beginning because arguments over financial matters must be avoided. Check the following:

   – the percentage rate of commission
   – variations for different origins of orders
   – basis of calculations for commission *eg* cif, fob *etc* (see page 65)
   – when commission is to be paid *ie* on receipt, delivery of an order or payment by customer
   – what happens in the event of a cancellation or bankruptcy of a customer?
   – dates by when commission is to be paid *eg* quarterly.

7. *Duration of contract* – you must state the date the agreement comes into effect – and the expiry date.

8. *Termination* – you must also state the provisions whereby the contract could be terminated before the natural expiry date *eg* breach of contract, bankruptcy.

9. *Language* – as you will be drawing up a contract which probably will be translated into another language, you must state which is the authentic text.

10. *Law* – the agreement should state which national laws govern the interpretation of the contract. Usually you will be able to state UK law (or EU provisions) but in some countries regardless of what is stipulated or agreed by the two parties, the law of the agent's country will apply.

These are by no means all the points to be discussed or agreed, but are listed to give you some idea what should or must be thought of.

Advice
When you are drawing up a contract with an overseas agent, seek the advice of a lawyer who knows the laws of the agent's country and trading style. It may seem costly but treat the sum as an insurance, because

the costs to you if things go badly wrong will be significant. Better to spend a little before doing the business than a lot later!

Motivating an agent

You must try to get as much attention from the agent for your product as possible. Here are some ways to keep your agent selling your product:

● Visit the market regularly as interest and support must be demonstrated. Make sure that you or a senior colleague make the visits.

● Help the agent make money and profit – suggest new ways of selling, new outlets to be developed, pass on enquiries, help with research *etc.*

● Help the agent prepare a marketing or sales plan and keep it updated.

● Communicate regularly with the agent with formal or informal reports covering results, information, changes in policy, product, personnel and so on.

Tip

No matter how well an agreement has been drafted, there will often be times when some difficulties will arise. Should this happen, the agreement should be interpreted in favour of the agent.

Your agent's goodwill is worth much more than the commission at stake in borderline cases.

SETTING UP A SALES JOINT VENTURE OVERSEAS

A joint venture – a scheme whereby you work, under a special agreement, with a partner abroad can be either one of the following:

● licensing

● franchising.

Licensing

The term licensing covers a wide range of agreements relating to the sale or leasing of industrial or commercial expertise by one party to another in return for 'valuable consideration'.

Items covered by licensing could include:

- a patent covering a process
- manufacturing know-how
- technical advice and assistance, even sometimes the supply of parts
- marketing advice or assistance
- use of a trade mark or name.

There are both advantages and disadvantages of entering into a licensing arrangement.

Advantages of licensing

- Market access – where markets are closed or difficult due to high duties, import quotas or prohibitions, freight charges or entrenched competition.

- Capital investment – licensing requires little capital investment and should return a higher rate of ROC employed.

- Licensee's local marketing organisation helps the licenser to make use of an existing distribution and sales set up.

Disadvantages of licensing

- Competition – when the agreement expires you will have an established competitor.

- Market exploitation – because the licensee will often not fully exploit the market potential – attracting competition – which means the licensor loses control of the marketing operation.

- Revenue – royalties usually between 2–7 % of turnover can often compare unfavourably with what might be obtained from a company's own manufacturing operation.

- Quality – control is often difficult and additionally the product may well be sold under the licensee's own brand name!

Finding, selecting and working with a good licensee will take time to produce results, but there is every good reason for such a venture to bring excellent returns and for an agreement to run for years.

Caution

Setting up a licensee-style operation needs probably more care and attention than does setting up an agent and the contract which sets out who is to be responsible for which aspects and contingencies (*eg* bankruptcy, tax, legal assignments *etc*) has to be given to a lawyer to prepare.

Franchising

Franchising is merely a form or licensing whereby:

● The franchisor provides a standard package of components plus management and marketing services or advice.

● The franchisee provides the capital market knowledge, personal involvement, premises *etc*.

Franchising is an excellent way to market products which are *not* patentable. Around the world franchising is enormous business and covers almost every category of market or product.

Example

Pepsi Cola relies heavily on franchising to market its soft drink. The franchisees own the bottling plants, employ staff, control their own advertising and promotion budget. Pepsi Cola sells its concentrates and provides promotional support and management advice to the franchisees.

Looking at the pros and cons of franchising

The pros and cons of franchising are broadly the same as for a licensing arrangement although franchise operations tend to be smaller. Finding good franchisees can be lengthy and costly but the concept allows good ideas to be rapidly developed. Obviously, licensing or franchising may not be an immediate method for your business to sell abroad but, with the rapid growth of franchising, you should know about what is involved and how franchising could help you break into new markets at relatively low cost.

HANDLING PERFORMANCE BONDS OR GUARANTEES

A great number of export opportunities come through **contract tendering** which is advertised internationally. If your business has any interest in tendering or bidding for the contract, you will be provided with a set of tender documents specifying the buyer's requirements and inviting price bids to be submitted to a stated authority.

Usually, the bidders are asked to demonstrate both commitment and ability to finance the deal by submitting either:

● **earnest money** – which is a percentage of the tender price or
● **bid or tender bonds** – which are legal documents in place of earnest money, issued by the bidder's bank.

If the contract is awarded, the successful bidder provides a **performance guarantee** in substitution for the bid/tender bond. This guarantee is passed via the bank.

Warning

● All bonds and guarantees are a real liability, so if you are required to provide a bond or guarantee of any kind, go and see your bank's international branch straight away.

● Do not agree to any form of wording until you have discussed the whole guarantee *etc* with your bank.

● Never submit a bid or tender for any work your company may have difficulty in fulfilling.

● Always find out in advance what bank charges and expenses will be in relation to the issue of bonds *etc* – your bank's and the overseas bank's charges *etc*. Build them into your contract price.

● Remember, a bond or guarantee is a contingent liability on your business until you are notified by your bank that it has been cancelled or has expired. *Never* just rely on your overseas buyer telling you – you must have official bank confirmation.

Different types of bond

There are a number of different types of bond but you will just need to know the basics of them:

● *Advance payment.* This is a guarantee which gives protection to the buyer who may make a payment to the supplier in advance of the contract being carried out.

- *Retention bonds.* These are issued to the buyer to allow him to release the final payment to the supplier. They also give the buyer security for **due performance** after the supply contract has been completed, or for a fixed period.

- *Warranty bonds.* These are issued to the buyer to warrant the performance of equipment for an agreed period.

If you have to submit such bonds or guarantees, *always* work in conjunction with your bank's international department.

3
Pricing for Export

The most difficult and most crucial decision a small business will have to take will probably be at what price to sell to customers abroad. This is usually a hard enough task for those selling into the domestic market, but with the extra dimensions of time and distance to consider as well, the problem becomes even more complex. However, this chapter seeks to simplify the process of decision-making.

Your aim is to try to obtain as high a **contribution** to your company's revenue from sales abroad as possible. How then can you price your goods to achieve this target?

CALCULATING YOUR REVENUE

Before you can even decide how to maximise your contribution to revenue, you need first to decide how you propose to *calculate* your revenue from selling abroad. **Revenue is not always the quantity of goods sold multiplied by their price**.

Example

2,000 items sold at £5 each would be £10,000 – but it is *only revenue* when you *receive the cash*. Now, if the goods had been sold to a customer abroad, you will probably not be paid for some while.

So, to the exporter revenue should mean **the financial results of sales made to export customers**. These should therefore be calculated in the same way for each sale abroad so that you can compare the results of selling to customers in different parts of the world.

Examining the three main methods of calculating revenue

● *Total revenue* – which is the full amount received for the goods you have exported, or the full amount you *expect* to receive at a later date. *Total revenue* is important when you look at cashflow, working capital required and the amount of credit you probably will have to give customers.

● *Ex-works revenue* – which is the total revenue from which has been deducted all the money paid to those people outside the company.

● *Retained revenue* – which is what is left from ex-works revenue after paying for materials *etc* bought from outside suppliers.

Retained revenue is the added value or return to the company for its own activity and shows what a company gets for what it spends. So, it has to cover all fixed and variable costs and whatever margin or profit or 'contribution' is made to the company's revenue.

BUILDING THE EXPORT QUOTATION

Whatever the pricing strategy you adopt, every price must be set with cost considerations in mind. The true cost of the goods in the market-place is at least a yardstick against which pricing decisions can be properly made. Some companies base their export prices on domestic prices plus suitable additions for freight, duty, insurance, mark-up and so on. The problem with following this route is that the domestic price usually contains elements which do not apply to sales abroad. By the same token, sales overseas will have costs not found in domestic markets.

The level of profitability of export sales has implications not merely for short-term profit, but also for pricing policy and overall marketing policy.

Note
It may be the case that an export price lower than the home market price is more profitable.

Assessing what price the buyer will pay

What should concern you most in arriving at a price is what price the buyer will pay (*ie* the end-buyer or user because the goods will have passed through several hands). This is not going to be easy to discover because the prices will vary in different parts of the world according to the factors influencing purchase.

Example
You wish to export handmade ornaments, crafted to a unique design. You need therefore, to ask the following questions:

1. Do people want handmade ornaments or would they be happy with mass-produced ones?

2. What value would potential buyers place on the ornaments – how much then would they be prepared to pay for them?

3. How would the price of your items compare with other handmade ornaments?

4. Do the buyers have the means of buying your products?

The answers coming back from various parts of the world would show that the rich in Florida would perhaps be prepared to pay more than the rich in Zurich. This example is intended to help you appreciate that you could lose profit because your price is too low, or lose business because your price is too high.

Advice
Concentrate on as few parts of the world as possible, so you may find that it is entirely practical as well as profitable to quote different prices according to where you are selling, as well as in what quantity, at what time and according to when you will be paid.

Always try quote in firm gross prices as customs officials are usually suspicious of discounts. Do not try and sell below your domestic prices ('dumping') and anyway it is unlikely to be worthwhile to do so.

PREPARING QUOTATIONS

So, having arrived at a basic factory price (to cover fixed and variable costs), you now have to consider how you will quote the price, which means deciding which of the international terms of delivery you will use.

Deciding which terms of delivery to use
Terms of delivery will inform the buyer what is included in your price, when and where delivery of the goods takes place and, most important, when title in them passes to the buyer who them becomes responsible for them. They also set out and define the duties of both seller and buyer. There are a number of these terms which have been defined and codified by the International Chamber of Commerce under the heading **INCOTERMS**. They define precisely what each term means so when using one or other of them you should add 'INCOTERMS 1990' to your quotation. (INCOTERMS are updated, revised, where necessary, every ten years.)

Here is a checklist that will help you avoid the more serious errors or omissions in calculating the profitability of your exports, including the most commonly used INCOTERMS.

- *Ex-works price*
  This is the most basic quotation you can give, which means that the buyer must collect the goods from you and pay all the costs to ship them (transport, insurance, duties *etc*) back to his own warehouse.

  If you sell this way, make sure you have included the cost of any special product modifications, and the appropriate company over-heads relating to the export order. This price will include agency commission, profit margin, export packing costs and a percentage of your export department running costs.

- *Free on board (fob)*
  This is undoubtedly the most common used terms of delivery because it allows the buyer the option of handling the insurance and transport himself. You, the exporter, provide all the documentation and pay for getting the goods loaded onto the selected method of transport.

  Fob is generally used for shipment by sea with a named port being added – *eg* Tilbury. If you are sending goods by air, then you use the term **FOA** (free on aircraft). For goods which are sent by a container through an inland clearance depot (**ICD**) the term is **FRC** (free carrier named point).

  Responsibility for the shipment passes to the buyer as soon as the goods pass over the ship's rail and he takes over the goods as well. Arrival at an airport or depot signals the moment when a buyer assumes responsibility.

- *C&F or cfr – cost and freight*
  Cost and freight means that the seller – **you** – pays all freight charges but *not* insurance. The buyer takes on all risks when the goods are on board ship or aircraft.

- *Cif – cost, insurance freight*
  Cif is the same as **cfr** except that insurance is paid as well by the exporter. It is also customary to add the destination port *eg* **cif Singapore**.

When talking about container shipments, the equivalent of the terms described above are:

- **dcp** – delivered carriage paid for **cfr**.
- **cip** – freight and insurance paid to a named point for **cif**, the seller's responsibilities remaining until the goods reach the **ICD** at destination.

One more important term to know about is **ddp** – delivered duty paid – which means the exporter pays all charges and carries the risks until the goods reach the buyer's warehouse.

Warning: Do make sure whether or not local VAT (for the EU) or its equivalent is included.

Selecting the delivery terms

The best advice is to quote as the customer requests, and you add on the extra costs as required under the terms of the delivery. If the buyer has made no request, then you choose how to quote.

Most exporters choose **fob** (free on board) simply because it gives a good deal of flexibility in delivery while many customers like it because they save foreign currency by using their own shipping line or doing their own insurance.

However, some exporters prefer to quote **cif** because they can earn extra by doing so and it helps earn extra foreign currency, if quoting in, for example dollars.

What else should you consider when building your export price?

● landing charges
● import duty
● internal distribution and storage charges, unless already covered
● distribution, wholesale and retail mark-up and local turnover or sales taxes
● credit costs
● forward exchange cover (see later)
● import paperwork – import certificate, consular invoice fees
● incidentals which can mount up and become almost another tax
● never forget all the one hundred and one sundries – for example:

    – small consignment handling/storage

    – service/repairs work

    – replacement part shipment (where goods are under guarantee).

It is surprising how much has to be added in – over and above the 'ex-works' price if you are looking to cover all the angles. Failure to address what may at first sight appear to be minor items could lead to loss-making at worst or low profits at best.

Quoting in a foreign currency

The first instinct of a new exporter is to quote prices in his own currency. This does admittedly provide two major advantages:

- It is simpler from the administrative point of view.

- The risk of any exchange variation is borne by the customer.

However, if your customer is not prepared to take such a risk, he will ask for a quotation on his own currency – eg US$ – so that *he* knows exactly how much *he* is paying for your goods.

When this happens you should comply. In order to avoid the risk of receiving less than you anticipated (due to currency fluctuation), you make a contract with your bank to sell the foreign currency forward and it is this rate you use in your quotation. Major international currencies can be bought and sold for several years ahead. If you do not use forward currency exchange, you could stand to make gains but equally you can end up making serious losses and few new or small exporters are knowledgeable enough to become currency speculators.

Local currency transactions are much better for importers, so make them whenever you can.

Beware, however, of the fact that a forward exchange contract does not offer complete protection against the exchange risk. The contract matures on a fixed dare, normally the date on which payment is due to be received from the buyer. If there is a delay in payment or – even worse – non-payment, the exchange risk is borne by the exporter. If you have insured the credit risk, then you will have no problem (credit risk insurance is discussed in Chapter 6).

Having decided which currency you are going to quote in, you have to decide the period of time the quotation remains operative, either by giving a specific date or by stating that the price will be that at the date of despatch – which, of course, is not particularly satisfactory, especially for the importer who may use your quotation to purchase foreign currency or to obtain an import licence.

Here is what you do. You make quotations, either by having a price-list or by stating the details on a *pro-forma* invoice. If you are quoting 'ex-works' or **fob**, you include details of the weights and estimated freight and insurance charges.

Adding your conditions of sale
Finally, to your quotation you will add your conditions of sale. You probably have these already for your own domestic market but for exports you should include:

- normal method of payment

- a reservation of property clause which retains your patent and other property rights

- a statement to the effect that the weights/dimensions are purely for transit purposes

- delivery dates are given in good faith

- damaged/defective goods will be replaced free of charge

- you hold your customer responsible for obtaining any import licences (*note*: some US importers/buyers may expect you to do everything – including checking and arranging import licences where necessary).

BARTERING

Sometimes you may find that you will be asked to take goods in payment for your goods – this direct exchange works for less-developed economies. However, the system presents many complications and is best left to experts to handle on your behalf.

On the other hand there are other forms of barter-style trading which, even if you do not become involved with them initially, you should know something about.

1. *Compensation trade* takes place where an exporter agrees to accept payment or part-payment in goods from the buyer's country in lieu of cash; but the deal is organised as two separate cash transactions, entered into simultaneously. Sometimes you will hear the expression **contra-trading** or **reciprocal trading**, which are all barter-type trading deals.

2. *Counterpurchase* is quite common. Here is how it work: an exporter is asked to buy goods from the importer in exchange for goods he has supplied – such goods representing some or all of the total value of the shipped order.

3. *Compensation/buyback* is where technical know-how, and maybe some equipment, is supplied by the exporter who then guarantees to buy back the finished product up to the total value of the supplied technology.

4. You may come across *switch trading* where the deal becomes a little more complicated as you, the exporter, will be eventually paid by someone in a third country.

> *Advice*
> **Counterpurchase** is the system you will most likely come across and it can be profitable.
>
> Unless the goods on offer are what you would normally buy, you will not want them. Your first step then is to consult a factor who will arrange to sell the goods offered by the importer. There are lots of such factors based in the City of London. What the factor does is to give you a price they will receive for the goods, less a commission of 15–20 per cent. By using this price you can then quote your products to the importer in terms of their goods.

Example
You sell one computer for maybe 20 cases of vodka (top grade). Your goods will be shipped to the buyer as per the factor's instructions, who pays you when he receives payment from the buyer. If you use a good factor you will avoid the risk and make the deal profitable.

Further tips on bartering

● Banks (or any of its alternatives) can help you access markets which otherwise may be closed to you.

● Be certain that such a deal is the only method open to you.

● Always try to get part of the payment in cash.

● Check in advance that you can either use or dispose of the barter goods offered.

● If the goods are going to enter the UK, check that they do not contravene UK import controls.

Case study

Compensation trade
The major consumer food and drinks manufacturer Cadbury-Schweppes used its international purchasing resources as a means of broaching the Eastern European markets. Its Swedish subsidiary manufactured tomato paste so the UK company accepted deliveries of Bulgarian tomatoes as part of its deal to sell its products into Bulgaria. Everyone came out of the deal with a WIN–WIN situation.

4
Organising Promotion Overseas

This chapter starts off with a warning! People will not buy goods from another country in preference to locally made products, nor will they buy from a totally unknown company, unless they are persuaded to do so.

There are, happily, many ways of helping overseas buyers and their customers to buy your products or services, without having to resort to financial inducement or bribery. However, in many places, bribery is a fact of life and so if you feel you have to resort to such activity, allow for it in your costs. Try though to make sure it is only paid *after* receipt of the order.

Make sure your company has a clear policy on this point and stick to it.

USING PUBLICITY MATERIAL

You will almost certainly need some literature for your overseas business just as you probably do for your home trade. Where possible try and use what you already have – leaflets, catalogues, instructions for use and so on. If this is not possible then you will have to adapt it.

Language
The text will have to be translated and for this you can go to a translation agency (the DTI has a list of such agencies).

Warning
The words cannot simply be *translated* into the other language – they need to be *rewritten* in the other language.

Always have the translated text put back into English by a third party to make sure that the correct meaning has been retained.

Example
The phrase used in one English brochure 'Out of sight – out of mind' was eventually retranslated back into English as 'Gone blind, gone mad'!

Advice
Stick to simple English for countries where it is appropriate and avoid any word-play or comedy which either has no local equivalent or will be totally misunderstood. Also check on your brand name (see earlier) or other expressions which even in English could give offence elsewhere. The USA uses American English (*eg* diaper for nappy, drapes for curtains, elevator for lift, bobby pin for hair pin), so it might be a good idea to get an American English/English English dictionary if you have sales and promotional material going to North America.

Illustrations
Make sure the illustrations are suitable, especially those of people, because it is so easy to show the wrong types.

Example
In Jamaica there are at least ten different degrees of colour, all typical of the multi-racial society. In such a situation it is best to avoid using people at all in illustrations.

Keeping illustrations simple
Try and use simple illustrations, particularly showing instructions for use since people abroad may not have a knowledge of English or a poor understanding of their own.

Design the literature for use at home and abroad at the same time because some languages take up more space (in words) than others. German takes some 25 per cent more space than English and you have to allow for languages (Arabic) which read from right to left – as well as the whole pagination make-up. Also, if you are selling to China or other countries where the type is vertical, you will need to accommodate this in your layout.

Advice
Be wary of excessive demands for your literature because customers habitually over-order. Also make sure you have its distribution in place before it is produced. There is nothing more disheartening that seeing your expensively produced literature gathering dust on a warehouse shelf instead of being properly and profitably used.

USING DIRECT MAIL

If you are considering a direct mail campaign, check first with a specialist direct mail house who has international experience. You need to work closely with them to ensure the correct salutation is used, lists are accurate, response mechanisms are correct and simple, and that local laws or controls are not contravened (*eg* data protection regulations).

The DTI will provide details of such agencies, who will be able to carry out the whole mailing process for you.

Advice

If direct mail is to be a major plank in your promotion programme, try and build and update your own mailing list. This then will be the most accurate of all.

However, only send out necessary information, because recipients will soon be turned off by too much mail and the scheme becomes counterproductive.

ATTENDING TRADE FAIRS, EXHIBITIONS AND SHOWS

Exhibitions are a regular feature of the business scene here in the UK but abroad they have an even greater significance for the following reasons:

● They play a generally more important rôle in the business plans of companies overseas than they do here.

● The ever-present problems of time, distance and cost in meeting customers and prospects are partially solved.

● Good product demonstrations overcome linguistic barriers.

● In some countries trade fairs are the only open way that face-to-face contact can be made with end-users' companies.

If you attend, for example the National Kids Fashion show in New York, the book exhibition in Chicago or the Miami trade fair to meet US store buyers, you can not only sell but also check prices, competitive products, new ideas and much more.

Advice
Check the following:

● Which exhibitions or trade fairs or shows are suitable: 'trade only' or 'trade then public' or 'public only'?

- Can you get DTI assistance in helping with travel, exhibition rent space *etc* (Fairs and Promotions Branch)?

- Where is the target audience?

- The timing of the exhibition – plus who organises it, how successful has it been, how well established is it, how big is it *etc*?

Checklist
Carry out a thorough check on your motives for going in the first place. Do you want to:

- take orders on the stand? ❑

- obtain leads/enquiries to follow up later? ❑

- merely generate publicity with a view to later business development? ❑

- meet prospective agents/distributors or talk to existing ones? ❑

- carry out a market assessment – will your product sell? ❑

Tip
Always:

- compare results to the original objectives
- check actual costs against budget
- follow leads promptly
- evaluate market data
- decide whether it is worth going again.

Case study
A direct selling and marketing company in the health market wished to expand its operation into Africa (East) and the Middle East. The DTI organised special terms for companies exhibiting in Nairobi and Teheran in Iran including transport of exhibition items, special rental terms of space, travel and accommodation.

The company decided that it had three main objectives:

- to sell its equipment on the spot
- to take enquiries to be followed up later
- to try and find suitable distributors for each area.

A by-product of all this was extensive media coverage in all the local newspapers, on TV and radio.

Not only did the company sell out all its stock shipped in for the shows, but a great number of enquiries were generated. Distributors were checked out and set up and were sold the enquiries that were generated as part of an agreed deal. Within two months both distributors were doing exceptionally well, with the distributor actually manufacturing some of the equipment in his own specially built factory and selling it under a licensing arrangement. Within two years the Iranian distributor had become one of the company's best operations.

Not all shows will produce such interesting results but it does serve to demonstrate that if you go out to see and be seen, you can achieve outstanding and unexpected results.

CONSIDERING STORE PROMOTIONS

The expression **store promotion** can refer to a variety of promotional activities with retail stores. In the international market scene, however, it is used to describe the more elaborate promotions staged in favour of consumer goods from one or more countries.

The long-term value of store promotions is hard to assess and there are as many opinions on the matter as there are people who express them.

Tips on store promotions

- Just as exhibitions, they should be part of an overall sales plan – not in isolation.

- The aim should normally be the ongoing supply of the products in the future – so any evaluation should take place about 12 months after the promotion.

- Promotions will usually be more successful if the products concerned are already being sold by the store.

- You may have to set up a proper distribution chain because, especially with food products, the goods will not normally be purchased directly.

- Any government assistance is granted to the promoting store, not the UK participating companies.

DEVELOPING PUBLIC RELATIONS

Never underestimate the value or power of well thought-through and executed public relations (PR). If you do not do it in-house, then there are many excellent PR companies who will be able to help you.

The UK is particularly well situated with regard to getting space in overseas media. There are around 700 correspondents of overseas newspapers, journals, radio and television based mostly in London. Overseas Trade Services of the DTI can provide a list.

The Central Office of Information (COI) will actually prepare a news release worthy of being submitted and circulated to relevant countries. The service is free and provides an excellent springboard into markets abroad.

Never forget the use of the BBC External Service which goes out in English and many other languages. What is of interest to the service are new products, sales successes overseas, exhibits at trade shows and technical research. Enquiries generated are passed to the company concerned.

Case study

A company working with the Royal National Institute for the Deaf designed and manufactured a new form of alarm based on a vibrating system (placed under the pillow and controlled remotely in a hospital or by a timer at home, it woke up sleepers who would never have heard an alarm).

The idea was so novel and distinctive that upon hearing about it, the BBC External Service interviewed the company's marketing chief to discuss its construction, ease of use, safety and so on.

Well over 20 enquiries were received from all parts of the world, mostly from companies who wished to have an agency of one form or another for the device – called 'Vibralarm'.

BUDGETING FOR PROMOTION

The amount of money you will have to spend promoting your products or services overseas will be restricted if you are a new or small exporter. Whatever the amount earmarked, you arrive at it in a logical way, so forget about thinking of a number, doubling or halving it and try to relate the revenue you hope to gain from your export sales to the amount of money that will have to be spent to obtain that revenue.

Even if you are working through an agent or distributor or with a department store group directly, there will be at least some financial input to cover promotions, promotional costs and maybe co-operative advertising. Many companies work on a percentage of sales to cover such costs. However, how do you decide the percentage? Figures can vary from 1 per cent to 70 per cent, which is not very helpful. Then you have to decide what to do with the budget generated this way – and, even if you have it, do you really need to spend it?

Advice

Forecast what it will cost you to win or gain a certain amount of revenue *from a particular territory. Then* decide if that amount of business is worth having from the point of view of its contribution to your overall business revenue.

This must be related to what you actually can afford to spend. As your exports grow you can determine whether a fairly similar percentage figure shows up for these territories.

Always, though, start as suggested then arrive at a budget which represents a sensible amount which the business could afford to risk and which will do the job expected of it.

Example

Exporting tools to Asia, with a budget of £5,000 to achieve a total revenue of £100,000, producing a gross revenue of £25,000 after all costs have been deducted. Three countries were nominated *eg* Singapore, Thailand and Malaysia.

To promote in local publications would cost £2,500 and visits to each country would cost a further £2,500, hence a budget of £5,000. Let us examine whether this is a justified amount.

Taking £5,000 from £25,000 leaves £20,000, the contribution to company revenue which is 25 per cent of the capital employed which was thought to be all right. £5,000 also works out at 5 per cent on the total revenue from sales, which is also a good amount, because industrial goods usually require between 1 per cent and 10 per cent of promotion. On the other hand, fast-moving consumer goods will normally require anything between 10 per cent and 50 per cent, which is probably way beyond your immediate ability.

Advice

Work out how much you think you need to produce the sales required or expected, then check the ratio of expenditure to revenue to see that it is more or less in line with what your sales will produce on a percentage basis.

If you are entering a new area you may find that you need to spend more money initially, in which case such expense can be allocated to capital expenditure.

Tip
Try to allocate all your promotion expenditure to specific territories so that you can monitor results from each more easily.

You will never ever have enough money to do everything that you want, so you must make the best decisions possible using your limited resources. Furthermore, you will never know whether you should have spent more or even less as you will never be sure of what you got for your money. Experience will eventually guide you.

Keep in mind what Lord Leverhulme said of advertising: 'I know that one half of my advertising budget is wasted – the problem is, I don't know which half.'

Advertising

It is unlikely that you, as a small or new exporter, will wish to advertise on a large scale but you will probably find that you may need to do some limited advertising in certain countries. Your first question to be answered is: 'How is the advertising to be handled?' The best answer is that you should never allow advertising to be done by your local agent or distributor because if you are jointly advertising it is usually a failure. In any case, if they are working on commission as an agent, advertising expenditure should not be their responsibility.

It is important for you to control every aspect of the advertising – the *amount* to be spent and *when* and *how* to spend it.

You should either use an advertising agent here in the UK who can advise you on the correct media and book space and produce suitable copy and graphics and pay the media on your behalf, or you can do it yourself which could pose problems, not least the time factor itself.

Advice

● Check the information your customers can give you for the most suitable media – including print, radio, TV and cinema, which in some countries is a very powerful media.

● Check yourself if you are abroad what your customers read or use themselves and so build up a picture of the most suitable vehicles for your advertising.

● Check very carefully what you say in your advertising message. For example, there is not much point in talking about labour-saving devices or advantages where or when labour is cheap. However, always stress the ease of machine operation – where labour is probably unskilled.

● Avoid slogans which are usually impossible to translate satisfactorily and use cartoons sparingly, if at all.

● Make your trade mark and brand name highly visible so that it stands out from local competition.

● Always get someone local to check your advertising before it is published or broadcast to avoid making silly gaffes or creating embarrassment.

Using gifts and samples

Gifts and **samples** will usually be asked for – so make up your mind at the start what your policy is going to be. Remember, though, that if not carefully checked, costs can mount rapidly. Therefore limit the distribution of either gifts or samples to customers of those agreeing to buy. This will generate publicity at low cost, but be warned – many samples are sold off locally! Use samples *sparingly* then at, for example, trade shows or store promotions.

As for gifts – anything useful for the office, pens, paper weights *etc* and even T-shirts and carrier bags, all bearing your name, will help promote your company name and products far more widely than can be imagined and at relatively low cost.

The success you achieve with your advertising does not rest solely on the budget you can afford. The *skill* of advertising and promotional work is to make 1p sound like £1 and this *can* be achieved through creativity, skilful media buying, planning, execution and monitoring. Linked in with good PR, you can make the **multiplier effect** work extremely well in your favour.

LOOKING AT ELECTRONIC TRADING

If you are planning to promote your products or business over the Internet, here are a few questions you should consider:

● Why should you use the Internet as opposed to any other medium?

- Who is going to be responsible for it?

- Is there an evaluation process to determine how well the Internet meets company needs?

- Is there any way you can check any cost/performance improvement?

- What will it cost to set up and maintain?

Examining the benefits of the Internet

You will be able to exchange E-mail with customers, prospects and colleagues, which is one of the best uses for the Internet.

- You can obtain **commodity codes** when preparing export documents.

- You can ask questions and get answers.

- You can send and receive documents.

- You can conduct business – send quotations and sell.

Costs should be reduced, efficiency improved and a better service given to prospects and customers.

Information can be made available to cover catalogues, production specifications, reviews of performance applications – indeed, anything which a company wishes to share with customers can be digitised and maintained at relatively low cost.

The **World Wide Web** provides traders with the opportunity to place an electronic catalogue advertising their goods allowing prospects to access details about types of goods available, their delivery, prices and payment terms.

Disadvantages of using the Internet

Many large companies use the Internet sparingly, if at all, and few are keen or even ready to entrust the main aspects of their **Electronic Data Interchange (EDI)** to the system.

There are three main reasons:

- security
- reliability
- control.

Payment over the Internet for international trade is not entirely 'bug free', although the boffins have come close to cracking the security problem. Once it is as secure as it can be then the Internet has enormous potential for facilitating international payments.

The EDI system

The EDI (Electronic Data Interchange) although currently only used by some major international traders, should eventually become more widely used amongst smaller exporters.

The benefit for users is that important data can be exchanged between the various organisations involved with your consignment *eg* customs, freight forwarders, shippers, banks and your buyer.

By only having to input data once, errors can not only be avoided by the initial self-checking encryption, but will not be repeated down the line by others who would normally have been using a manual paper-chase system. Furthermore, information relating to delays on ships or aircraft diversions can be made to all parties, making tracking and control much more effective and cost saving.

Once more organisations join in the EDI process, the more useful it will be to all international traders. Details of EDI and 'paperless' trade can be obtained from SITPRO, the Simpler Trade Procedures Board, who advise on simplifying the preparation of export documentation through the use of aligned documentation systems. SITPRO is an independent agency, part funded by the DTI (see Useful Contacts section). Prepare one master document for each transaction and from that master produce all documentary requirements. 151 Buckingham Palace Road, London SW1. Tel: (0171) 215 0825. Fax: (0171) 215 0824.

5
Shipping Goods Abroad

Having received some orders from overseas and prepared them for despatch or shipment, you will need to decide which is the quickest and most effective system to use, assuming that your customer has not told you previously.

DECIDING ON YOUR METHOD OF TRANSPORT

There are a number of considerations if you are left with the choice:

- speed
- cost
- security/safety
- damage potential
- packaging requirements.

All these issues will be discussed later when the actual method of transport has been decided. The five most commonly used primary methods of transport are:

- sea
- air
- road
- rail
- parcel post.

Naturally a combination of some of these is used ultimately to deliver to the end customer or user.

Using sea transport

Most goods go by sea. This is because ships provide the cheapest method of transport. Ships carry heavy and bulky loads at relatively low cost. However the price you pay for this is slowness. Add to this the distance a customer may be from the port and the time taken for a consignment to be delivered home can be considerable.

One major development in sea transport in the last decade has been the introduction of container ships – that is, ships specially built to carry containers. Because such ships spend less time loading and unloading their cargoes, the time spent in transit is greatly reduced.

When you ship goods in containers, you either use a full container load or, if you have only a small shipment, your goods go in the container with those of other exporters. You do not deliver to the sea port but to the container port (ICD).

A further development in shipping which has also helped reduce transit time and that is the ro-ro (roll on, roll off) ferries, which means you use road or rail transport in conjunction with sea transport as one system or operation.

Using air transport

Although as much as 75 per cent or more of the world's trade goes by sea, more and more is now being air freighted. The reasons for this are:

- it is quick
- goods require less packing
- goods stand less chance of being lost or damaged.

An important point often lost on exporters is that smaller quantities mean less money being tied up in 'stock in transit' plus the fact that speedier delivery means quicker payment.

The downside is the cost. Also the fact that air cargo is limited by size or what the aircraft can accommodate. The goods most suitable for air transport are perishable foods and flowers, highly seasonal goods, emergency (medical) supplies, spare parts and, indeed, any high value goods which need to be in transit for the shortest possible time.

Nowadays, of course, the Channel Tunnel has speeded up the movement of people and goods between the UK and mainland Europe and the ferries have begun to feel the competition quite severely, although the airlines have not.

Air cargo is carried on most passenger flights and you can book space on them in the same way as you would book passenger accommodation. You have to make special arrangements, of course, for unusual cargoes *eg* valuable items, live cargo, unusual shapes or sizes or those which demand particular attention.

Using road transport

The most significant advantage of road transport over the other methods is that it offers door-to-door delivery.

For the smaller exporter who may not have sufficient for a complete load, the operator offers a **groupage** service whereby a freight forwarder **consolidates** the shipments of several exporters which saves freight costs, as well as providing a regular service to principle cities.

With the Channel Tunnel, the time factor is not much slower than by air and much less expensive.

Using rail transport

There is an excellent rail network throughout Europe which is now linked to the UK through the Channel Tunnel. This network is made up of a highly sophisticated network of cargo trains made up of containers, privately-owned wagons and train-ferry wagons organised on a groupage basis.

Rail *can* be quicker than road – especially to the further corners of Europe and for longer distances. Over short-haul distances the time factor is less obvious. Rail is also reliable and is probably subject to less delays that air or road.

Rail Parcel Service is a further option with the costs including documentation, handling and customs processing charges.

Using parcel post

The parcel post service operated by the Royal Mail (Post Office) is often overlooked by exporters. The service uses surface or air transport to destinations all over the world.

There are restrictions as to size and/or weight as well as contents, but items can be handed in over post office counters or can be collected for a door-to-door service.

For simple export packages/parcels sent to a number of diverse destinations, this service could be ideal. Details are available from the *Post Office Guide* and *Royal Mail Overseas Compendium*.

Using couriers

This is a fast-growing service worldwide with the major players in it operating their own aircraft, ships, trucks and vans. They tend to specialise in personal deliveries office-to-office (or airport-to-airport) of small items *eg* documents, artwork, spares, samples, computer tapes, films, medicines and so on.

Each courier operator will have its own regulations or restrictions, but if sheer speed door-to-door is essential, then such a service would be hard to beat, with next-day delivery promised.

ASSESSING COSTS OF FREIGHT

Sea transport rates

Even If your freight forwarder is going to handle your shipment, you should know some basics about how cargo is assessed and costed so that you can both take an interest in and be aware of what is being done on your behalf.

Conference lines (*ie* regular, timetable sailings) have fixed tariffs. If, though, you ship regularly by a conference line ship, you will be entitled to a rebate of around 10 per cent.

For a **non-conference ship** (*ie* better known as a **tramp** which pick up and sail with anything, anywhere) you will usually pay less but have to haggle over the rate – and of course you will not know when the ship will sail.

Sea freight rates are based on weight or measurement – whichever is the higher. So always weigh your goods in kilograms. Also measure them in centimetres and then cube the result.

What shipping lines do is to compare the weight with the volume on the basis of one cubic metre = one metric tonne = 1,000 kilograms. To turn cubic centimetres into cubic metres divide by 1,000,000. So goods 3.2 cubic metres but weighing 2.8 metric tonnes will pay 3.2 times the freight rate.

- Most cargoes are larger than they are heavy.

- Rates obviously vary according to destination *and* by type of goods and there is usually a minimum rate.

- Freight is also usually paid in advance.

- Freight is usually quoted in US dollars.

Air transport rates

Charges for air cargo are fixed by IATA, the International Air Transport Association, and most lines' charges are similar. Airlines obviously work more by weight than size and they use a ratio of 7,000 centimetres to one kilogram, so airlines charge consignments by weight rather than volume.

Road and rail transport rates

Both these systems are highly competitive but rail rates are standard – but with regular Channel Tunnel users, negotiable – varying according to destination and type of goods. Rail uses the same ratio (weight to volume) as sea transport.

You and your freight forwarder should carefully assess which system, or combination of systems, you should use because the wrong choice could affect the profitability of your exports (if your customer has left the shipping to you to handle).

There is little point in airfreighting goods which are not wanted for a couple of months which may end up in a warehouse costing your customer money in storage charges.

PACKING GOODS FOR EXPORT

Just how you pack your goods will also affect your transport costs since there are special container rates – for full and less than full container loads.

Packing is now a highly specialised function in exporting and you would be well advised to consult a specialist such as Frazer International of Colnbrook near Slough, who not only is a freight forwarder, but also a specialist packer. Odd or difficult sizes, shapes and weights present few problems.

What do you need to consider in your packing?

- Liability to damage or loss.

- The type of transport being used – with goods going by sea usually needing more than those going by air. Road transport may save packing compared with rail which may increase the need for it.

- You must comply with local (*ie* destination) regulations. For example unless timber used in packing has been impregnated, and certified, it may not be used in shipping goods to Australia.

- Take note of climatic conditions – extremes of heat or cold could harm the products.

- If you are sending 'dangerous goods', you will need to pack and label them accordingly. Figure 1 is a sample dangerous goods note.

Marking consignments for export

Whichever system you use to ship goods, you must mark the consignments with the name and address of the consignee – but to prevent theft *never* state the contents. By ship you use the internationally accepted method of showing:

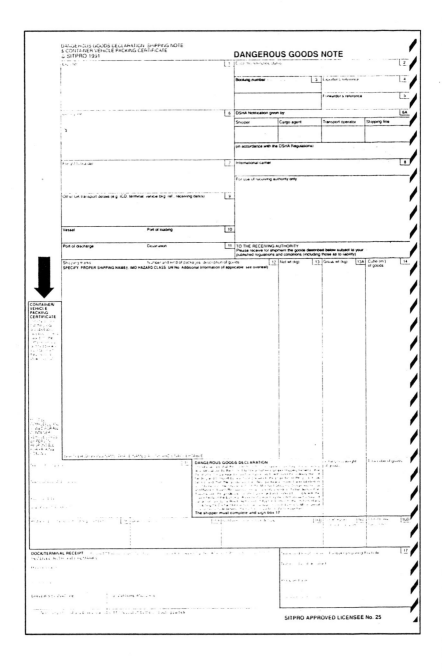

Fig. 1. Dangerous goods note.

- order number
- destination
- name or mark of the consignee
- number of packages in the consignment *eg* 3 of 15.

It is customary to add weights and measurements in centimetres and kilograms. A packing list for the consignee can be included so that he can identify the contents of each package.

UNDERSTANDING TRANSPORT DOCUMENTS

Sea transport

You begin with a simple **booking form** for sending goods by ship. Shipping lines have their own forms or you can use a **standard shipping instruction form**. See Figure 2 for an example of this.

Next will be a **standard shipping note (SSN)** which must go with the goods when they are sent to the docks. You keep one copy and send the other five with the goods. One of these will be returned to you without any comments if the goods arrive in the same condition as described by you. See Figure 3 which illustrates the SSN.

Basically, the SSN acts as a receipt for your consignment from the port authorities. It is also an instruction to the docks as to what to do with the goods. It also enables the port authorities to charge you for handling the goods, charges you have to pay if you are shipping **fob**.

Then you will see a **bill of lading** which the shipping line will issue to you once the ship has sailed with your goods on board.

Bill of lading

- A **bill of lading** acts as a receipt for the goods and if they are 'in apparent good order and condition' you will get a 'clean bill'. If not in good condition, you will get a 'dirty' or 'claused bill', and the shipping line will not admit to any liability as to their condition when off-loaded. See Figure 4 for an illustration of the bill of lading.

- The bill of lading acts as a contract of carriage between you and the shipping line.

- The bill of lading acts as a title to the goods – the goods will only be delivered to the person holding the original bill. If you withhold this you can prevent delivery taking place.

Export Cargo Shipping Instruction *(facsimile)*

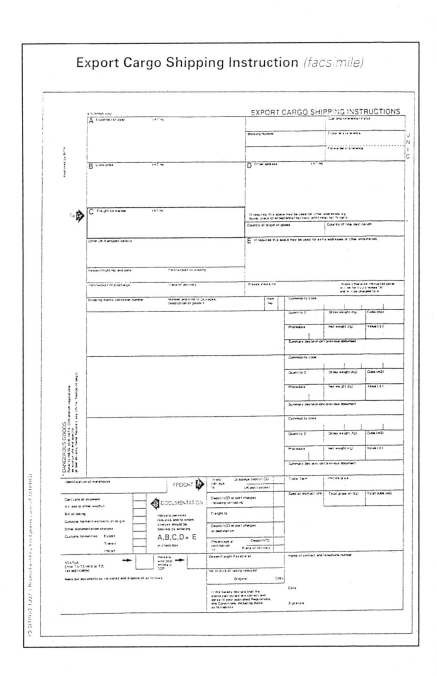

Fig. 2. A standard shipping instruction form.

STANDARD SHIPPING NOTE - FOR NON-DANGEROUS GOODS ONLY

IMPORTANT USE THE DANGEROUS GOODS NOTE IF THE GOODS ARE CLASSIFIED AS DANGEROUS ACCORDING TO APPLICABLE REGULATIONS SEE BOX 18A

Exporter 1

Customs reference/status 2

Booking number 3 | Exporter's reference 4

Forwarder's reference 5

6

Freight forwarder 7 | International carrier 8

For use of receiving authority only

Other UK transport details (eg. ICD, terminal, vehicle bkg. ref. receiving dates) 9

Vessel/flight no. and date | Port/airport of loading 10

Port/airport of discharge | Destination 11

The Company preparing this note declares that, to the best of their belief, the goods have been accurately described, their quantities, weights and measurements are correct and at the time of despatch they were in good order and condition; that the goods are not classified as dangerous in any UK, IMO, ADR, RID or IATA/ICAO regulation applicable to the intended modes of transport. 10A

TO THE RECEIVING AUTHORITY - Please receive for shipment the goods described below subject to your published regulations and conditions (including those as to liability).

Shipping marks | Number and kind of packages; description of goods, non-hazardous special stowage requirements 12 | Gross wt (kg) of goods 13A | Cube (m³) of goods 14

For use of Shipping company only | Total gross weight of goods | Total cube of goods

PREFIX and container/trailer number(s) 16 | Seal number(s) 16A | Container/trailer size(s) and type(s) 16B | Tare wt (kg) as marked on CSC plate 16C | Total of boxes 13A and 16C 16D

DOCK/TERMINAL RECEIPT Received the above number of packages/containers/trailers in apparent good order and condition unless stated hereon.
RECEIVING AUTHORITY REMARKS

Haulier's name

Vehicle reg. no

DRIVER'S SIGNATURE | SIGNATURE AND DATE

Name of company preparing this note 17

Date

(Indicate name and telephone number of contact)

630 Non-completion of any boxes is a subject for resolution by the contracting parties.

Fig. 3. A standard shipping note.

Bill of Lading *(facsimile)*

Bill of Lading for Combined Transport shipment or Port to Port shipment

Shipper

B.L. No.
Booking Ref.:
Shipper's Ref.:

Consigned to the order of

P&O Containers

Notify Party Address

Place of Receipt

Vessel and Vry. No.

Place of Delivery

Port of Loading

Port of Discharge

Marks and Nos; Container Nos;	Number and kind of Packages; description of Goods	Gross Weight (kg)	Measurement (cbm)

Above particulars as declared by Shipper, but not acknowledged by the Carrier (see clause 11)

Total No. of Containers Packages received by the Carrier

Movement

Freight and Charges (indicate whether prepaid or collect)

Received by the Carrier from the Shipper in apparent good order and condition (unless otherwise noted herein) the total number or quantity of Containers or other packages or units indicated in the box opposite entitled "Total No. of Containers Packages received by the Carrier" for Carriage subject to all the terms and conditions hereof (INCLUDING THE TERMS AND CONDITIONS ON THE REVERSE HEREOF AND THE TERMS AND CONDITIONS OF THE CARRIER'S APPLICABLE TARIFF) from the Place of Receipt or the Port of Loading, whichever is applicable, to the Port of Discharge or the Place of Delivery, whichever is applicable. Before the Carrier arranges delivery of the Goods one original Bill of Lading, duly endorsed, must be surrendered by the Merchant to the Carrier at the Port of Discharge or at some other location acceptable to the Carrier. In accepting this Bill of Lading the Merchant expressly accepts and agrees to all its terms and conditions whether printed, stamped or written, or otherwise incorporated, notwithstanding the non-signing of this Bill of Lading by the Merchant.

Place and Date of Issue

Number of Original Bills of Lading

IN WITNESS of the contract herein contained the number of originals stated opposite has been issued, one of which being accomplished the others to be void.

For the Carrier:

As Agent(s) only.

ICS
CTBL
April 78

024687

Fig. 4. Bill of lading.

90

Shipper's Name and Address | Shipper's account Number

Not negotiable

Air Waybill

issued by

Copies 1,2 and 3 of this Air Waybill are originals and have the same validity

Consignee's Name and Address | Consignee's account Number

It is agreed that the goods described herein are accepted in apparent good order and condition (except as noted) for carriage SUBJECT TO THE CONDITIONS OF CONTRACT ON THE REVERSE HEREOF. ALL GOODS MAY BE CARRIED BY ANY OTHER MEANS INCLUDING ROAD OR ANY OTHER CARRIER UNLESS SPECIFIC CONTRARY INSTRUCTIONS ARE GIVEN HEREON BY THE SHIPPER, AND SHIPPER AGREES THAT THE SHIPMENT MAY BE CARRIED VIA INTERMEDIATE STOPPING PLACES WHICH THE CARRIER DEEMS APPROPRIATE. THE SHIPPER'S ATTENTION IS DRAWN TO THE NOTICE CONCERNING CARRIER'S LIMITATION OF LIABILITY. Shipper may increase such limitation of liability by declaring a higher value for carriage and paying a supplemental charge if required.

Issuing Carrier's Agent Name and City | Accounting Information

Agent's IATA Code | Account No.

Airport of Departure (Addr. of first Carrier) and requested Routing

| to | By first Carrier | Routing and Destination | to | by | to | by | Currency | CHGS Code | WT/VAL PPD COLL | Other PPD COLL | Declared Value for Carriage | Declared Value for Customs |

| Airport of Destination | Flight/Date | For Carrier Use only | Flight/Date | Amount of Insurance | INSURANCE - If carrier offers insurance, and such insurance is requested in accordance with the conditions thereof, indicate amount to be insured in figures in box marked 'amount of insurance' |

Handling Information

SCI

| No. of Pieces RCP | Gross Weight | kg lb | Rate Class / Commodity Item No. | Chargeable Weight | Rate / Charge | Total | Nature and Quantity of Goods (incl. Dimensions or Volume) |

Prepaid | Weight Charge | Collect | Other Charges

Valuation Charge

Tax

Total other Charges Due Agent

Shipper certifies that the particulars on the face hereof are correct and that insofar as any part of the consignment contains dangerous goods, such part is properly described by name and is in proper condition for carriage by air according to the applicable Dangerous Goods Regulations.

Total other Charges Due Carrier

Signature of Shipper or his Agent

Total prepaid | Total collect

Currency Conversion Rates | cc charges in Dest. Currency

Executed on (Date) at (Place) Signature of issuing Carrier or its Agent

For Carrier's Use only at Destination | Charges at Destination | Total collect Charges

ORIGINAL 2 (FOR CONSIGNEE)

Fig. 5. Air waybill.

91

These three aspects of a bill of lading are the most important that you should know about – but remember they come in sets – with so many originals and so many copies, so decide how many you want when you make them out.

Air transport
Air waybills are made out by the airline and you will be sent a copy with the others going to the carrier and consignee. They are not titles to the goods but act as a receipt for the goods and as a contract of carriage only. See Figure 5.

Road and rail documentation
The **CMR** (Convention de Merchandises per Routes) and the **CIM** (Convention Internationale de Merchandises) are made out by the carriers, and act as receipts and contracts of carriage.

The reason that air waybills and the CMR and CIM do not act as title to the goods is that the goods will be delivered direct to the consignee.

Parcel post
For goods going by parcel post, a receipt will be issued which acts as a contract of carriage, and as delivery is made direct to the consignee, it does not act as title to the goods. What you could do however is to instruct the local postal service to collect payment before delivering them.

UNDERSTANDING CUSTOMS PRACTICE

Many people develop a mental block when it comes to handling anything to do with Customs. They need not as we shall see, because by following a simple route, this aspect of getting your goods abroad can be made relatively pain free!

Customs and Excise Authorities all over the world control both the imports and exports of their respective countries.

When you export you will become involved with Customs on two occasions:

- when goods leave this country (or wherever you are exporting from)
- when they arrive in their country of destination.

Explaining the function of customs authorities
There are three main functions of Customs authorities:

1. They control the flow of goods in and out of the country.

2. They raise revenue by charging duties on imports and sometimes on exports.

3. They record the movement of goods entering or leaving the country so that the government knows its balance of trade *vis-à-vis* the rest of the world.

Most goods from Britain can be freely exported. There are some which require an **export licence** *eg* drugs, war materials, some chemicals, atomic energy materials and antiques which are deemed to the part of the national heritage.

Note
All goods exported from the UK must be identified by a **commodity code** and this should be shown on all Customs and transit documents.
For goods *going into* the EU you use a variation of the Harmonised (Coding) System called TARIC but basically HS (Harmonised System) and TARIC are similar.

Note
Exporters are legally responsible for classifying their goods correctly. Even if a freight forwarder or other party has prepared documentation on the exporter's behalf, the exporter remains liable and could be penalised if goods are wrongly classified.

Obtaining Customs notices
Exporters should obtain Customs notices:

- 827 (EU Preference Procedures)
- 828 (covering rules of original – which is extremely important)
- 829 (other preference-giving countries).

These are obtainable from local Customs and Excise Advice centres. Even though you may work with a freight forwarder, you should know how they can help you and your business.
Export licences can be obtained from the Export Licensing Branch of the Department of Trade and Industry.
The reason your goods must be carefully classified is to allow the correct import duty to be charged by the Customs in the destination country. A Commodity Code Tariff booklet is available from local Customs and Excise offices.

Trade within the European Union

No Customs declarations or clearance is required for goods traded within the EU member states, as basically they are not 'exports'.

However, there is a new system for collecting statistics on the trade in goods between EU countries – Intrastat:

● a community-wide system

● its requirements are similar in all EU countries

● businesses not registered for VAT or private individuals who move goods within the EU do not have to bother

● only the supply of goods *between* EU countries is covered

● supply of services is excluded

● it does not cover trade outside the EU.

More specific details are available from HM Customs and Excise offices who have a booklet, *A General Guide to Intrastat*.

Trade with the rest of the world

For goods being sent outside the EU and to countries which have a preference trade agreement with the EU, you should know about the **EUR1 Customs form** which is used for goods shipped to:

● EFTA (European Free Trade Association) countries *ie* Norway, Switzerland and Iceland

● other countries covered by special trade agreements *ie* Cyprus, Israel, Malta

● a number of former Comecom (economic association of communist countries) states in Eastern Europe where again a number of special agreements have been signed (see Customs and Excise for details). See Figure 6 for an example.

An **EUR2 form** is needed for postal consignments up to £1,850 in value (see Figure 7). Turkey is a special case as it has joined the Customs Union. **A. TR. form** is used to determine the status rather than the origin of the goods. If you are trading with Turkey, seek special help anyway.

MOVEMENT CERTIFICATE

1. Exporter (Name, full address, country)

EUR1 No. S 1904506

See notes overleaf
before completing this form.

2. Certificate used in preferential trade between

THE EUROPEAN COMMUNITY

and

(Insert appropriate countries or groups of countries or territories)

3. Consignee (Name, full address, country) (Optional)

4. Country, group of countries or territory in which the products are considered as originating
EC

5. Country, group of countries or territory of destination

6. Transport details (Optional)

7. Remarks

(1) If goods are not packed indicate number of articles or state "in bulk" as appropriate

8. Item number: marks and numbers | Number and kind of packages (1): description of goods

9. Gross weight (kg) or other measure (litres, cu m., etc)

10. Invoices (Optional)

SPECIMEN ONLY

(2) Complete only where the regulations of the exporting country or territory require

11. Customs Endorsement
Declaration certified
Export document (2):

Form............. No............

Customs office..................

Issuing country or territory:
UNITED KINGDOM

Date ....

(Signature)

Stamp

12. Declaration by the Exporter

I, the undersigned, declare that the goods described above meet the conditions required for the issue of this certificate

(Place and date)

(Signature)

C 1299   Page 1 FCO (December 1996)   1

Fig. 6. EUR1 Customs form.

Before completing this form read carefully the instructions on the back

FORM EUR 2 No. 983771

1 | For use in preferential trade between the EEC and (insert the appropriate country – see Note 1 overleaf).

2 | Exporter (Name and full address, including country)

3 | Declaration by the exporter.
I, the undersigned, the exporter of the goods described below, declare that the goods comply with the conditions under which the form may be issued and that the goods qualify as originating products under the provisions governing the preferential trade shown in Box 1

4 | Consignee (Name and full address, including country)

5 | Place and date

6 | Signature of exporter

7 | Remarks

8 | Country of origin

E E C

9 | Country of destination

10 | Gross weight (kg)

11 | Marks and numbers on packages; description of goods

12 | Authority in the exporting country responsible for verification of the declaration by the exporter.

HM Customs and Excise
Customs Directorate
Division H Branch 4
Dorset House
Stamford Street
LONDON SE1 9PS

Printed in the UK for HMSO Dd56960 7501 10/88 45282

C1297   CD 0404 N2(4:88)   F 4143(OCT 1988

Fig. 7. EUR 2 form.

96

MOVEMENT CERTIFICATE

1. Exporter (Name, full address, country)	A.TR.1 No.A 1183737
	See notes overleaf before completing this form

2. Transport document (Optional)

No .... date ....

3. Consignee (Name, full address, country) (Optional)

4. **ASSOCIATION**
between the
EUROPEAN ECONOMIC COMMUNITY
and
TURKEY

(1) Insert the Member State or Turkey

5. Country of exportation | 6. Country of destination (1)

(2) Insert where appropriate "Compensatory Levy Turkey"

7. Transport details (Optional) | 8. Remarks (2)

9. Item number

10. Marks and numbers; number and kind of packages (for goods in bulk, indicate the name of the ship or the number of the railway wagon or road vehicle); description of goods

11. Gross weight (kg) or other measure (hl, m3,etc.)

12. CUSTOMS ENDORSEMENT | Stamp

Declaration certified

(3) Complete only where the exporting country requires

Export document (3)

Form .... No ....

Customs Office: ....

Issuing Country: ....

....

Date ....

.... (Signature) ....

13. DECLARATION BY THE EXPORTER

I, the undersigned, declare that the goods described above meet the conditions required for the issue of this certificate.

Place and date ....

.... (Signature) ....

C 1232   CD 1028-1-N6(1G-88)   F 3948)   OCTOBER 1988   )

Fig. 8. ATR form (layout agreed between the EU and Turkey).

97

Advice
Apart from understanding what Customs and Excise does and why, you should have some knowledge of the mechanics of such matters as LEC (local export control) whereby you can have goods cleared and declared at your own warehouse; also PE/E or period entry (exports) which allows you to declare to the Customs via computer-produced media.

The simplified clearance procedure (SCP)
One final system which may be of interest to regular exporters is the simplified clearance procedure (SCP), a pre-shipment system whereby you are given a CRN (Customs registered number) which provides the evidence that you (or your freight forwarder) will make the final declaration.

The Single Administration Document (SAD)
If you ever have to use it, it will be for non-EU countries. It is a document which makes filling in forms of various types, for various purposes 'simple' in that all the information is produced in one set of data; each sheet of the set is used as and when required, saving time, money and errors.

UNDERSTANDING VAT REQUIREMENTS

Apart from Customs and Excise concerns, small or new exporters may not quite understand if or how VAT may impact on their businesses. Here is a very quick guide.

All goods sold are subject to UK VAT charge except in the following cases:

● For sales to buyers in the EU member countries, *if* the buyer's VAT registration number is shown on the exporter's invoice, VAT is not chargeable.

● For sales to buyers in countries outside the EU, invoices can be zero-rated and UK VAT is not chargeable.

● For sales to private buyers in the EU member countries UK VAT is chargeable (*eg* mail order business).

Note
All VAT-registered businesses must complete two (extra) boxes on their VAT returns showing:

- value of goods supplied to EU countries
- value of goods acquired from EU countries.

Also exporters are required to show adequate records to ensure that all VAT and INTRASTAT statistics are accurately and correctly recorded.

USING FREIGHT FORWARDERS

Many exporters may feel intimidated by the welter of documentation, paperwork and other items when it comes to the actual shipping of their hard-won export orders. While a good number learn the ropes and handle their own paperwork, a great many small exporters prefer, for one reason or another, to allow a third party to assume responsibility for this part of their business. What used to be a shipping and forwarding agent is, today, termed a freight forwarder.

Benefiting from the services of a freight forwarder

The work of a freight forwarder will include:

- advising you of any special requirements regarding the marking of your cargo

- the packing of your cargo

- any Customs requirements overseas in respect of documents

- working out the best route for the shipment – most economic routes and obtain the best rates

- booking space on your behalf and paying for it, since most freight is payable in advance

- arranging transport to the docks or airport, or arranging for the proper instructions to be passed to your own transport people.

Provided you supply him with the basic information about the shipment, he will make out the standard shipping note (SSN) and Customs entries.

As a regular 'exporter', he will probably have his own CRN (Customs registered number) therefore being able to declare goods on your behalf – which could be a great advantage if you only make infrequent exports and do not have your own CRN.

Looking at what else your freight forwarder will do

● He will make out and have signed the various transport documents
  – *eg* bill of lading, and will despatch these as you want.

● He will also handle the SAD as well as special invoices or
  certificates of origin.

● Your freight forwarder could even insure the goods for you.

Some forwarders now operate their own road services to Europe, others have their own containers; most will offer consolidations by air and can offer small exporters very good rates.

What does the service cost?
You will probably pay for the services rendered between 3 per cent and 5 per cent of the total freight costs, so while the forwarder wants to increase the amount of 'commission', he will be forced to offer competitive rates to keep the business. He will also charge out-of-pocket expenses and document expenses in addition.

Selecting a freight forwarder

Call the British International Freight Association (BIFA) for a list of members (see Useful Contacts). Membership requires the provisions of a high-quality service with evidence of the employment of qualified personnel, together with liability insurance cover and conformity with the Association's Code of Conduct.

Check the prospective forwarder thoroughly. You want someone efficient who does not regard your business as too small to bother about, but on the other hand much depends on how you are going to treat the selected forwarder and the service and information you give him.

Think very carefully about what you really need from your forwarder and how you can work with him. A good forwarder can become an extension of your business and a 'partner' in all but name.

If you become so experienced in handling export shipments, you may think that you could do it for less money. Before making such a decision, work out all the pros and cons and cost them.

Advice
For new or small exporters, who ship out infrequently, use a freight forwarder. The benefits to you override any drawbacks. Only if and when

you become big enough, with regular shipments, could it become more cost-effective or efficient to have the work handled in-house, and even then the answer is not always clear cut.

Case study

A company based in North Wales, because of a number of tax and other incentives, shipped out its products to Europe, South Africa, the Middle East and Australia. Such was the amount of traffic that the transport department, already stretched to maintain deliveries throughout the UK, passed all its overseas business to a local forwarder. With the necessary instructions prepared in advance of the call to collect, the forwarder was able to relieve the transport department of all overseas worries, allowing it to maintain a trouble-free service in the UK.

A more efficient and thorough service was provided to all customers in the UK and abroad at a modest charge to the company. The company decided not to use a third party for UK deliveries since they felt they would lose flexibility and control.

KNOWING ABOUT PRE-SHIPMENT INSPECTION

There are a number of countries who demand that an inspection of the goods is carried out prior to shipment. Most of these countries are in Africa, but Mexico, Bolivia, Pakistan, Philippines, Peru, Indonesia, Ecuador, Bangladesh and Haiti also expect pre-shipment inspection (PSI) to be carried out. This is done by their appointed agent.

Understanding why PSI is required
PSI is carried out in order to prevent:

- over-invoicing
- supply of sub-standard or counterfeit goods
- supply of secondhand for new goods
- supply of obsolete goods for current types
- discrepancies – quality or quantity
- concealed commissions or interest charges
- evasion of custom duties.

Advice

- Never underestimate or try to ignore the requirement for pre-shipment inspection of your goods.

- Immediately you are advised of a PSI requirement, contact the inspection agency to check on the requirements and the timescale involved.

- If you are unable to resolve differences with any pre-shipment inspection agency, you may appeal in writing here in the UK and in the importing country.

One important point you must watch out for is: who is to pay for the inspection, and for the repacking of the goods if they have to be opened up?

6
Getting Paid

One of the biggest worries facing a small or new exporter is that you might not get paid. This simple fear is probably responsible for the fact that more UK businesses do not or will not export.

It is an understandable fear! Who is to say a buyer thousands of miles away, in a strange country, with a different language, customs and laws is either able or likely to pay?

You may get a status report which says the buyer has the funds, but this does not guarantee you will still be paid.

TAKING SENSIBLE PRECAUTIONS

Such fears are needless or groundless if you take sensible precautions to prevent this happening, from the very beginning of the transaction. This section will show you not only how to protect yourself against non-payment, but also how to make it easier for your customer to pay you.

Invoices

The basic document used in export is an invoice, but whereas people pay against invoices here in the UK, in the export trade invoices are used mainly as a record of the goods shipped and a statement of the terms on which they have been shipped.

A commercial invoice contains details of weights, marks and measurement plus details of freight and insurance costs and the method of despatch. Such an invoice will only be used in payment if you are giving your customer **open account** terms (*ie* you trust your customer to pay without any other documentation being necessary on the due date). However, in many countries payment may not be made against an invoice but rather against a **bill of exchange** or **draft** (see later).

You will need to send customers a number of copies of your commercial invoice with each shipment, the exact number depending on the customer's local needs. You will probably have heard of a *pro forma* invoice, which is no more than an invoice used for making quotations –

PROFORMA INVOICE

Invoice Number	
Customer Order Number	Customer Account Number

Invoice Address

Bankers

National Westminster Bank Ltd
52 Threadneedle Street
London EC2R 8AL
Code
Account Number

Country of Origin of Goods	Country of Destination
Terms of Delivery and Payment	

Vessel/Aircraft etc.	Port of Loading
Port of Discharge	Insurance

Marks and Numbers: Description of Goods	Quantity	@	Amount (State Currency)

	TOTAL	

We hereby certify this invoice true and correct

Signatory & Status of Authorised Person
Place and date of Issue
Signature

Fig. 9. A *pro forma* invoice.

104

with the words *pro forma* written on it (see Figure 9). Where payment is to be made in advance, it would be used to get payment from an importer.

Note
Payment in advance is obviously the most satisfactory way of being paid. If you can get payment before you even buy raw materials to fulfil the order, you will be even better off.

Defining the function of an invoice

Invoices are used for Customs purposes when the customer receives the goods. They are therefore certificates of value and origin. Sometimes the commercial invoice need only be signed by the exporter to be accepted by the importer's own customs as a true declaration of value and origin on which Customs duty will be paid.

Elsewhere the declaration of the exporter will not be enough and so a **certified invoice** will be required. This then becomes a certificate of origin – sometimes requiring to be certified by a local Chamber of Commerce. Some South African countries require a **consular invoice** and you get the form from the relevant embassy and have it signed by an official once you have completed it.

The invoice is the first document you will have to prepare – your freight forwarder cannot do this for you, although he may be able to obtain and prepare all the other certificates of origin required.

To sum up, invoices are a means of knowing how much you require to be paid as well as advising the importer what has been sent to him, and to get those goods through Customs.

Note
You will normally pay for invoices to be stamped by Chambers, embassies or consulates. As this takes time, allow for this when you supply all the necessary documents to the bank against a Letter of Credit (see page 106).

Cash in advance

From your standpoint, as mentioned earlier, this is ideal for you because you have the money and the goods (if you have actually made them). However, from the importer's point of view, this is not the best arrangement because he has parted with his money and has no guarantee he is going to receive the goods.

Where the customer is unknown to you receiving the 'money up front' is probably a sensible idea and you would be justified in asking for payment in advance. Payment should be made against either a commercial or *pro forma* invoice, the money being sent to you by cheque. Prudently you would clear the cheque before despatching any goods.

A **banker's draft** would be more satisfactory because it is a cheque issued by a bank. They are not normally used however because of the risk of theft. Payments are made generally by mail or electronic transfer – even using Internet or the bank's own computerised system for transferring money, called SWIFT (Society of Worldwide Interbank-Financial Telecommunications).

Always offer a discount for payment in advance but beware those buyers who offer a deposit with the balance on arrival of the goods, because he may not pay that balance, so getting goods at a discount.

Documentary letters of credit

Many exporters, especially new ones, begin to worry about Letters of Credit because they imagine them to be complex and costly affairs. They *can be*, especially when you hear that around 60 per cent of them are returned by the banks for errors or omissions, which delays the timetable and costs money.

However, they are really quite simple. An importer asks his bank to open a credit in favour of an exporter. He lays down certain conditions under which the exporter is to be paid, normally that the goods are to be despatched according to his instructions and that the documents needed to get delivery are provided.

What happens next is that the *importer's* bank advises the *exporter's* bank of the credit and, provided everything is in order, they pay the exporter accordingly.

From the importer's point of view this is satisfactory as he knows that the goods will be shipped according to his instructions and that he will not have to pay for them unless this has been done. From your point of view you know that, if everything is conducted according to those instructions, you will be paid. This however, makes two assumptions:

● that the credit is *irrevocable ie* it cannot be altered without the consent of the four parties concerned

● that it is a *confirmed* credit which means that the money has been credited to a bank in your country and that the money will be paid to you. If the credit is unconfirmed, it is still in the importer's bank. Circumstances could arise whereby that credit might not be transferred to you.

Advice
Only accept a *confirmed* credit and, in addition, make sure it is confirmed by a reputable bank, because the only time you will not get your money is if that bank goes bust. Better not to take chances even if the chances are remote.

Checking a letter of credit
When you receive a letter of credit:

● Check it carefully to make sure you can comply fully with all its conditions.

● Make sure that the goods you are going to supply match *exactly* what is written or described on the credit.

● Check the total amount of the credit to see that it covers all that you expect to receive because, while you can be paid less, you cannot be paid a penny more.

● If a shipment date is specified, check that you can ship before that date.

● Make sure you will be able to obtain all the documents required before the expiry of the credit – because nothing is paid if the credit has expired.

Don't leave anything to chance!

Example
If a full set of shipped on board bills of lading is specified, check what is meant by a full set because opinions differ as to how many originals and how many copies make up a full set.

Another item to check
Some countries may not accept certain shipping lines for political or economic reasons, so it might be worth a quick check before committing your exports. If you have checked it through and found it acceptable, you can accept it. However, if you find anything in it which you disagree with, you must get the importer to amend it immediately. Also make sure changes are to the importer's own account.

Questions and answers
Who gets a copy of the credit?
Those responsible for producing, packing and shipping the goods plus your freight forwarder, if you have one, as well as those preparing the documents, insuring the goods and handling the credit with the relevant bank.

What happens next?
Having despatched the goods and gathered all the documents specified in the credit, you take these to the advising and confirming bank with a draft drawn at sight (see later) and you will be paid.

This means you will be paid after the goods are shipped but before they arrive, depending on how far away the importer is. There are strict rules governing documentary letters of credit, being an internationally recognised method of arranging payment for goods and services.

Different types of credits
They are issued subject to the uniform Customs and practice for the issuance of documentary credits – best known by a publication reference UCP 500 and issued by the International Chamber of Commerce in Paris – but copies can be obtained from the London office (Tel: (0171) 823 2811) or Chambers of Commerce or Bank International branches.

There are several types of credits which you may well come across and might even want to use:

● **Revocable** – this type of credit can be changed or cancelled by the buyer or the bank at any time until payment. *Advice*: avoid this type of credit.

● **Irrevocable** – this type of credit means that the terms and obligations *cannot* be altered without the agreement of *all parties* to the letter of credit, which includes the seller. If a letter of credit does not state whether it is revocable or irrevocable, it will automatically be considered irrevocable.

● **Unconfirmed** – this is where the seller is reliant on the issuing bank's undertaking and ability to provide the funds when payment is due.

● **Confirmed** – this is where the advising bank adds its 'confirmation' guaranteeing that, provided all terms and conditions are met, payment will be made no matter what happens to the issuing (buyer's) bank. A charge will be made by the confirming bank for giving this added protection.

To summarise, therefore, the best type of credits are **confirmed, irrevocable letters of credit**. You may come across other forms of credits. Here are just some, with a word about how they operate and how they could help you in your overseas business:

● **Transferable** – which allows for all or part of the advice to be transferred to another supplier. They are therefore a very useful way of sourcing goods from third-party suppliers and ensuring they meet the terms and conditions of the prime credit. They are *irrevocable*.

● **Revolving** – these are useful where regular shipments are to be made to the same buyer. They can 'revolve' either on a time or value basis and they avoid repetitive single-valued shipment letters of credit. They also ensure that documentation requirements are constant for all shipments.

Other forms of letters of credit are **standby** and **back-to-back**. The standby letter of credit is used as a form of trade debt guarantee, used as a back up to allow trading on 'open account' terms.

Note
Around 80 per cent of all world trade is conducted on open account terms. *Back-to-back* credit – the seller's *export* letter of credit – is used to *back* a further credit to the seller's own supplier.

The subject of letters of credit – or whichever description is given to them – is of necessity quite complex and only a very simple guide has been given, enough to illustrate how you should determine which type of letter of credit may be best for your trading needs. For more detailed explanations on letters of credit, it would pay you to speak to your local Chamber of Commerce or the international division of your bank.

Advice

● Watch the costs carefully – they could erode profits considerably.

● Watch charges for amendments, faxes, instructions *etc* and make sure they are for your buyer's account.

● Many international traders prefer to handle the letter of credit from their end so that they are in control of what is happening at all stages instead of having to respond to changes.

Bill of exchange

A bill of exchange is often referred to as a **draft**. The simplest form of a bill of exchange is a cheque, which most of us use in everyday life. A bill of exchange, just like a cheque, can be prepared on virtually anything (even a cow was once used and table linen too from restaurants), but plain or company letterhead paper is used although pre-printed format Bills are available.

Basically, a bill of exchange is a demand for payment, to be settled on demand or at a fixed or determinable future time. From a customer's point of view, opening a credit in favour of an exporter means he has to tie up his money and, in many cases, pay before he receives his goods. He may, therefore, prefer to pay after he takes delivery.

From the exporter's point of view, you may want to allow credit to your overseas customers but at the same time you will want to be paid in full, and when expected. A bill of exchange will allow this to happen, especially if you are shipping goods by sea. Or you can use the bill of exchange to withhold delivery in the event of non-payment by the importer.

How a bill of exchange works
Earlier a bill of exchange was described as a **draft**, which it is in the initial stages – drawn on a customer by you, the exporter. So it is in fact the opposite to a letter of credit because you, as the exporter, draw the draft and send it to your bank with instructions to forward it to a correspondent bank in your buyer's country.

This bank then presents the draft to the importer. If he agrees to pay either then or at a later date, he is handed the relevant documents to allow him to take delivery. Even if goods are not shipped by air, a draft can still be drawn on a customer because it is a legal document demanding payment. If it is refused, you, the drawer, have legal backing to obtain payment.

Two types of draft which you should know about

● sight
● term.

A **sight** draft means that it is payable 'at sight' by the person on whom it is drawn. When the bank in your customer's country receives the sight draft, it presents the draft to the importer and when he pays he gets the delivery following receipt of the documents.

A **term** draft is payable at so many days – in multiples of 30 days *after sight*. The local bank presents it to the buyer and if he agrees to pay on the due date, he writes 'accepted' on it when he is given the documents, to enable him to take delivery. The importer's bank then returns the draft to the seller's (your) bank – it has now become a bill of exchange – who sends it to you.

You then can do either of two things with it:

- retain it for full payment by the importer
- discount it for cash which means you receive most of the money quickly, the cost to you being the discount (or commission) taken or charged. This could help your cashflow and reduce interest on borrowings.

With bills of exchange, as with letters of credit, you should talk to the international department of your bank, who will advise you when setting up such a payment system.

Comment
Both letters of credit and bills of exchange seek to protect the buyer and seller by trying to find a system whereby goods and payment can be safely exchanged so that both parties to the deal are happy with every aspect of it and that no-one feels at risk through either non-receipt of the goods or non-payment for them.

Open account trade
Over 80 per cent of the world's trade as mentioned earlier is handled on **open account** basis. When you know your overseas customers very well you may wish to allow them to pay you on this basis. If you do you should lay down the terms on which you expect to be paid – and these will be contained in your conditions of sale *eg* one month following receipt of the goods.

In such a case you can safely send all documents directly to the buyer/importer so that he can take delivery. If there is doubt about his ability to pay, you can insure against this possibility (see Chapter 7) but of course this helps the buyer more than you and it does give you only very slight protection. So you should use such action with caution.

Warning

In a number of countries payment will not be made against an invoice so you could be asked to draw a draft (as above) for the amount, payable on a due date. Such a draft will not be used in connection with the documents. France is just such a country, as French customers always pay this way.

It is an excellent way of dealing with business conducted on open account because no-one should have any objection to a draft *if* he has every intention of paying you on the due date anyway.

APPOINTING A THIRD PARTY TO COLLECT PAYMENT

We have now looked at a number of ways in which you can be paid for your exports and you must select which method you use, which is most efficient, effective or simple for you and perhaps acceptable to your customer.

However, you may decide that the whole business of collecting your dues is too much to handle and wish for a third party to take over your debtor's ledger. Here then are three options which could offer you some alternatives.

Factoring

As a small or new exporting business factoring could well be of interest. It is a way of leaving the collection of money from your customers to a factoring company. This company becomes *totally* responsible for collecting the money and paying you. There is an Association of British Factors and most factors are controlled by the banks.

How factoring works

All you do is to hand over your export sales accounting function to a factor, who not only checks the buyer's credit status, but also collects the money. They will generally guarantee 100 per cent payment to you – even if the importer has not paid.

Questions and answers
What are the benefits of using a factor?

It saves you a heap of clerical work, allowing you to concentrate on what you do best. It also eliminates foreign exchange risks and lets you trade on open-account terms without risk of non-payment.

What is the cost to the export business?

You will most likely have to pay somewhere between 3-3.5 per cent of collectibles but this translates into less probably than it would be for you to have your own export accounting system.

Are there any other benefits?
Often factors operate in pairs, one here in the UK working with other companies overseas. The UK factor takes care of your ledger while the overseas 'associate' checks status, collects the money and takes the risk if payment is not made. Some factors even provide shipping or forwarding services.

The other benefit is that you could expect up to 75 per cent of money due from the factor as soon as they are advised. Do not imagine however, that you get this at no cost – you will pay several percentage above bank rate so it can be quite expensive to raise cash this way. However, if you need the cashflow, it is one option to study and cost out.

Even regular and old overseas clients can get into financial trouble and exporters can lose money as a result so, with so much business being conducted on open account, factoring has a number of attractions that should be studied seriously.

Forfaiting

Many people confuse **factoring** with **forfaiting** and while there is some similarity, forfaiting has a number of major differences from factoring.

Forfaiting is the term used to discount or forfait a bill of exchange. If you are an exporter of capital goods and have to give long-term credit, then you should know about forfaiting. What happens is that you sell the total amount of what you are owed to a forfaiter for a discount. You are then paid the discounted amount – so you have no more worries that the buyer will not pay you for part of the contract. Now the importer must have a reputable local bank to guarantee payment, but the forfaiter collects over the period of the contract.

In effect, forfaiting is similar then to factoring but on a much larger sale and beyond the scope of factors.

Invoice discounting

Invoice discounting is very similar to factoring but it operates at lower costs because the discounting house never involves itself with the collection of payments.

Invoice discounting provides finance for an agreed period of time, usually to the end of the period of credit you have allowed your buyer.

As you can see, there are numerous ways in which you can arrange to be paid and ways by which you can receive some of your money more quickly than others. What you will always have to check though is that:

● your customer is creditworthy or solvent
● your payment channels are well set up and secure
● your goods are not released until either you have been paid or you are confident that you will be.

Remember – a sale is just a gift until it has been paid for.

THINKING ABOUT FOREIGN CURRENCY

Spot and forward rates

In Chapter 3 we talked about foreign currency quotations and why it was usually best to quote in your customer's own currency. Now you will discover how you can make this work for you and how foreign exchange risks can be avoided.

By whichever method your customer pays you, he will be paying in his own currency because that (usually) is all he has. If then you quote him in sterling, you leave him to take the risk that by the time he comes to pay you, it may cost him more than he expected when you negotiated the contract and he accepted your quotation. By quoting him in his own currency he knows *exactly* what he is going to pay.

Now *you* take the risk, because when he pays you in his currency, it may not be worth as much as when you quoted him because the exchange rate may have moved against you. Of course, if the rate of exchange moves the other way, you will gain. As you are an exporter of goods, though, and not an expert in foreign currency, you should not really be involved in such risks.

Rates of exchange are published daily and quote the average buying price of the day before. This rate is what you buy from the bank.

Example
If £1 equals $1.67, this means when you sell pounds and buy dollars you will have that amount of dollars. Your US customer will have to buy pounds to pay your account by selling dollars to his bank, a little more actually than the $1.67, to allow for charges.

What are spot and forward rates?

● **Spot rates** are rates for deals concluded on the spot.

- **Forward rates** are for deals to be done at some time in the future. **Forward** rates are **spot** rates at a premium, which means they will be lower than the spot rate or at a discount, which means they will be higher.

  Forward rates will be quoted for at least up to six months ahead. They will vary according to whether the deal is to be made on a specific date or during a specific time, for example, one or three months, in which case they become known as 'options', a business in its own right.

What you should do

If your customer wants a quotation in his own currency and you do not want to receive less when it is converted into sterling, you should make a forward contract to sell the foreign currency to your bank – either on a particular date or between certain dates on an option basis. Then you will be quoted by the bank the appropriate forward rate and a guarantee to pay you the equivalent amount in sterling at that forward rate.

Example

Spot rate for dollars is $1.67 – **forward rate** is $1.63. On a £10,000 order you could quote $16,300 instead of $16,700, which makes your price much more attractive and competitive. You could on the other hand keep the difference and increase the profit.

Note

Only quote customers in their own currency if there is a forward market for them.

By the same token if you are buying from overseas, you can make similar contracts with your bank to buy a foreign currency forward at the forward rate. This will let you know exactly what you are going to pay in sterling, eliminating any risk of paying more than you have intended.

While you cannot profit from any favourable rates of exchange, your prime objective is not to make profit on exchange movements but to trade profitably and securely.

CHECKING AND CONTROLLING CREDIT

If you are going to trade on anything apart from cash with order, or in advance, which involves being paid at a later date, you should, prudently, establish a procedure for assessing your buyer's ability to pay. Very similar in fact for those of you who have been trading in the domestic market.

Some important points, however, must be established:

● Any procedure adopted must be applied automatically to every new customer.

● Every buyer's creditworthiness should be effectively established using the best and most up-to-date processes and/or agencies.

● Every customer's account with you must be regularly reviewed and updated.

● Note every delay in late payment on your buyer's records and the reason. Every delay costs money and will reduce your profit margin on the deal.

● Credit limits can be reduced as well as increased to reflect the amount of business activity and payment record of customers.

● Produce a list regularly showing the debt age of all outstandings and chase up overdue accounts or tell customers that you cannot supply further goods until their overdue accounts are settled or brought more up to date. This will bring the sales team into conflict with the accounts team, naturally. However, if the customer is looking increasingly financially unsound, why should you continue to increase the size of his debt to you with an even greater prospect of non-payment?
  Sales and accounts people should get to know their customers well enough to prevent this situation ever arising. If there is a genuine reason for non-payment, you must consider carefully goodwill in the equation of doing long-term business.

● Effective credit control procedures should reduce the risk of incurring everyone's nightmare – **bad debts**.

What new exporters should do
Always ask for and receive the name and address of your customer's banker(s). This is *vital*. Then make sure the bank(s) is capable of handling the international financial and trade transactions. Your own bank will advice you of their status. (This should be done electronically.) *Your* bank will need to know:

● full name and address of the buyer's banker, if not already known or checked

- what you are enquiring for – *ie* the amount and for how long – so that they can determine whether they are trustworthy for that sum and time. You *may* obtain a general standing and for credit up to so much outstanding at any one time.

Some advice re credit

- If you are going to trade on regular, monthly terms, you may start to supply a second or third month's shipment before you are paid for the first consignment. *Take care*!

- Always enquire for more than you require *ie* for more than the value of the order, as this will probably give a better indication of the buyer's credit standing.

- Do not forget that your bank will charge you for status enquiries – but treat these as good *insurance* payments.

- Never rush to supply goods – and always wait for and consider the response you receive from your bank concerning the credit status of your customer.

- If you are unhappy with the terms of the reply you get, check everything over with your bank's international department.

- Beware of the buyer who places reasonable-sized orders and pays without problems over a period of several months and then places and outstandingly large one. Whilst it does not indicate that there is anything untoward about the business or ability to pay, there should always be an extra degree of caution if such a situation arises, with maybe some payment structure set up in advance so that in the event of a problem, you have recourse through some mechanism. Of course, if the buyer is fraudulent and simply disappears with the goods without paying, then you have a problem unless you have some form of credit insurance (see Chapter 7).

- You can, and perhaps should, use a reporting agency which may be able to give more detailed information for you *eg*:

  - details of ownership where known
  - last filed balance sheet information
  - credit/payment record
  - description of business activities

- record of any charges over assets
- details of the principals' other business interests – which could be very revealing, depending on the nature of your own business.

See Useful Contacts at the end of the book for some agencies to contact.

● British overseas Commercial Posts will provide written reports covering:
  - trade interests and scope of activities
  - territory covered
  - other suppliers represented
  - warehousing and distribution
  - sales strength, after-sales support.

This is extra but invaluable information which you should perhaps know about if you're going to trade regularly using credit.

Final warning!
Always know the costs of giving credit, which means the giving up of interest on your own funds for so many days or months, costs of monitoring debts *eg* telephones, faxes, correspondence or other electronic media and the bank's charges as well.

Build sufficient margins into your quotation to cover these points. Then you should maintain your expected return or profit level.

Remember – when dealing with credit, **check** and **control**.

RAISING MONEY FOR EXPORTS

You may be able to finance exports out of your own resources. It is more likely, though, that you will have to finance some or even all of your exports from outside the company. In the short term this could be done in a number of ways but, before you consider any of them, you should refer to a credit risk insurance agent – the one you select will depend, usually, on the length of credit period you require and the amount to be covered. However, as mentioned earlier, there are several ways to raise money to finance your overseas trade.

● Overdraft. You may obtain an overdraft from your bank but it will probably be at a prohibitive rate, possibly making your quotation uncompetitive as you have to price in the bank's charges.

● On the other hand, if you have a credit risk insurance policy (see Chapter 7) you are more likely to be granted a loan because the bank will know that the insurance company will pay even if your customer cannot or will not. In effect you are providing some security for the loan for which you will be granted a special rate of interest, the amount being decided by international agreement.

● If you have agreed with your customer that he pays by a confirmed, **irrevocable letter of credit,** and therefore do not need credit risk cover, you can use the letter of credit itself as security for a bank loan. If you also have transferable credit (which allows for all or part of the value of the credit to be transferred to another supplier), you can use this to pay your own suppliers and also pay yourself when the goods are shipped.

● If you are to be paid by a **bill of exchange** (a demand for payment) you may get it discounted and take the cash by selling it to a discount house (who then collects the full amount from the buyer). If you have **credit risk cover** you will get an even better deal as the discount house knows the insurance company will pay if the customer does not.

Note
These methods are based on raising money in cases where you need short-term credit, probably for less than 180 days, because normally letters of credit or bills of exchange are used when the customer will pay within that period.

Banks' schemes for exporters
A further way of raising capital to finance exports is via the bank's own scheme. All banks have their own scheme which they offer to export customers. It is worth checking with your own bank to see what they can offer you – terms, period, advance limits *etc.* While you may not think you could qualify, it is worth a call to the European Investment Bank (EIB) of the EU which has a number of schemes to help small businesses, either with direct loans or with loans from other banks.

Factoring
Remember also that if you use a factoring company to collect payment from your customers, the factor will advance some or all of the money outstanding. Beware of this system for raising money as this tends to be a more expensive way than others.

On the other hand, if you deal with confirming houses, they could help you finance your exports because they pay you in sterling when you supply the goods. You have no risk of non-payment and all your paperwork is done for you.

Forfaiting
Forfaiting has already been described as well but, as was mentioned, this method is used for more capital and long-term projects which may not suit the smaller business exporter.

Debt collection

● If a buyer regularly delays payment, check to see whether your credit and payment terms need revising.

● Check whether the buyer has advised any details of faulty goods, missing goods, damaged goods or even complained of late delivery. Two questions should be asked if any of these points apply:
  – Were such circumstances advised to you promptly?
  – Are any issues still under discussions which could (legally) delay payment?

● Check copy invoices – were they completed fully and accurately with payment terms clearly set out?

● If you have an agent use him to press for payment.

● Contact the buyer by telephone, fax *etc.*

Note
A good idea is to call them a week before payment is due to make sure that everything is in order and that you will get paid on time and in full. A great deal can be learned from the way the conversation goes! After all, it is *your* money you are claiming. If the debtor claims to have paid or to have instructed his bank to make payment, check the date, bank name, ask for reference numbers and follow everything through. Any overdue accounts should then be paid by using SWIFT – telegraphic transfer – to your bank account, even though the original terms were different.

Using a debt collection agency
If none of the above produces results, you may decide to use a debt collection agency.

Collecting debts in different countries can produce headaches. If you go to court to enforce payment you must be prepared to spend not only a lot of time, but also a considerable amount of money. Legal notices will favour the debtor and remember the language problem you will encounter as well. Hiring local legal help is, of course, one way round this but his charges are likely to be high.

Finally, you may well win your action but getting the money (which is why you went court in the first place) will be another matter altogether. Better by far to go to a **debt collection agency**. You will need to go to one which has international connections, offices or associates, who can handle the collection in the problem country. First, check on their fee or commission rate and then put every document *etc* in their hands so that they are fully aware of all the issues. INTRUM JUSTITIA is such a company, with offices in many parts of Europe.

Case study
A UK company was commissioned to carry out some research into various commodity markets for a US-based client. The work involved not only the research side, but also the preparation of a report using the findings.

The UK company invoiced the US organisation but nothing was forthcoming, not even an acknowledgement.

After repeated attempts, the UK company asked the US Embassy here in London for the names of debt collection agencies in the city where the US company operated. One firm was contacted by telephone, the details given and rate of commission agreed.

Within three weeks the debt was collected. Whilst the net amount remitted to the UK (in US$) was nowhere near the original amount expected, especially after exchange charges were made by the bank, the fact was that 70 per cent of something was better than 100 per cent of nothing.

Alternatives to debt collection agencies
If you do not have a debt collection agent, you might like to check the following:

● Your bank's international branch should be able to obtain information from either its own branch in the country or through an approach to its correspondent bank.

● The Regional Office of the DTI, using the services of the British Embassy or High Commission in the debtor's country.

● You can also contact your own Chamber of Commerce who may well liaise with its sister organisation in the debtor's country.

Advice
Monitor credit periods and payment performance; take early action to contact any overdue customers and stick rigidly to your payment terms. **Any move away from your terms will be taken as a sign of weakness which will be exploited in future deals. Start as you mean to go on.**

You will be respected for your firm stance and you will avoid doing business with slow or non-payers as a result.

7
Guarding Against Failure

ALLEVIATING THE RISK FACTOR

Being in business at all involves *some* risk. Being in the exporting business however, exposes you to higher risks than those encountered in the domestic market.

As a small or new exporter you will not be able to afford failures so it is only sensible to guard against them as far as possible.

The first period of inevitable risk is *during transit* to your overseas customers when goods are in danger of being lost or damaged. Therefore, you should have the cargo insured.

Cargo insurance

The subject of cargo insurance warrants the advice of a good marine insurance broker. He will not only arrange for your cargo to be insured when it is sent overseas, but will also explain some of the implications of cargo insurance to you.

Although there is no law which says cargo *has* to be insured, the **responsibility** for seeing that the goods are insured rests with their **owner**.

First, you should establish who is to insure the consignment. The terms of delivery on which you sell will determine or define who the owner is. For example, in an **fob** contract the exporter is the owner up to and until the goods go over the rail of the ship – thereafter the importer is responsible. In a **cif** or **cip** (cost insurance freight and carriage and insurance paid to) contract, it is the seller's responsibility to insure.

What happens in practice, however, is that goods are usually insured on a **through basis** – that is, from the time they leave the exporter until they reach the importer.

It is up the importer to say, when placing an order, if he will insure it or if he wants you to arrange the insurance on his behalf. Therefore always ask what the importer wants if it is not stated on the order. If he is paying by letter of credit, this will probably be specified as part of the conditions. Here are some simple facts that you should be aware of regarding the insurance of cargo:

- You cannot insure any cargo in which you have no interest. Apart from your interest in the cargo your customer as the eventual owner, also has an interest, and interest can be placed onto whoever becomes the eventual owner.

- Remember that the carriers or handlers will also have an insurable interest because they could suffer if the goods were to be lost or damaged while in their possession.

- You will insure goods for a stated sum known as the **insurable value** and this should be such that in the event of a total loss of the goods, their owner (whoever that is) on being paid this insurable value would be exactly the same position as he would have been had the loss or damage never occurred.

Calculating insurable value

'Insurable value' is usually calculated on the **cif value** of the goods *plus* 10 per cent of that value. The 10 per cent represents compensation for the cost of replacing the goods *or* to cover the inconvenience of being without the goods.

- **Total loss**: You receive the full insurable value.
- **Partial loss**: You receive a proportion of the insurable value.

If the goods are damaged and the cost of restoring or repairing them would cost more than their original value, this is known as **constructive loss**. Insurers will pay full insurable value to whoever has the rights to the damaged original goods.

Deciding which risks to insure against

It is up to the owner of the goods to decide which risks to insure against and, provided such risks are specific – *ie* **definable** – virtually any risk can be covered. However, there are two main exceptions:

- You cannot insure against **inherent vice**, that is damage that cannot be avoided, *eg* salt or sugar attracting damp.

- You cannot insure any illegal cargo.

Other exceptions are:

- poor packaging

- unseaworthiness, where known or suspected

- delay, *eg* by strikes or

- financial losses – not covered, however caused.

Case study
The French truck drivers' strike of November 1996, when Channel ports and main routes were blockaded, caused enormous problems – human as well as cargo-related. The UK government sought compensation from the French government for losses stemming from such activity as it was unlikely that insurers would cover losses.

LOOKING AT DIFFERENT TYPES OF INSURANCE

The types of insurance you can take out have been defined as **Institute Cargo Clauses A, B and C.**

- **Clause A** is virtually 'all risks'.

- **Clauses B and C** are basic cover, only to be used when goods are unlikely to be damaged.

All these exclude **war risks** and any damage from **strikes, riots** or **civil commotions** which have to be specifically added. There is nothing to stop you adding any number of additional risks if you want. Premiums are not that high but depend on the nature of the cargo, the packing and destination and, of course, the risks against which it is insured. As a general guide you could plan to pay £1 for every £100 of the insurable value.

Advice
To keep down premiums, use a good packer, freight forwarder and first-class shipping lines.

If you are a regular exporter, it would be impractical to take out a separate policy for every consignment. You can, under *'the principle of utmost good faith'*, take out some form of **open cover** or policy. The benefit of this is that the insurers will agree to cover all your shipments without being told in advance what they are, *provided* you tell them when they are to be made. If you do this you can issue your own insurance certificate.

Remember, insurance certificates form part of the total shipping documents so by endorsing the certificate claims may be made by the importer, or anyone with an insurable interest in the goods.

Making a claim
Hopefully, you will never have to make a claim, but if you do remember the following:

● Advise your broker or insurance company immediately any loss or damage is known and provide as much information as you can to support your action.

● Follow the advice proffered by your broker or insurance company.

● Treat all insurance matters as **urgent** – top priority. **Never delay**.

One final point – insurance policies or certificates should be endorsed by the insured to make them a 'bearer' document, which means that any claims can be made by the buyer in his country.

LOOKING AT CREDIT INSURANCE

Having protected the cargo with insurance, you should now look at ways of protecting *yourself* against risk of non-payment. You may have some credit insurance covering customers or clients in your domestic market. However, if overseas customers fail to pay there are added complications. For example, getting your hands on the goods and shipping them home will not usually be an alternative.

Covering credit risk is as important as insuring your premises, plant, stock *etc*. Your customer's debt is possibly your most vulnerable yet most important asset – the money owed to your business is needed to continue trading. There are a number of companies who specialise in covering credit risk. The main providers are:

● NCM – for cover up to two years

- COFACE – short to medium cover – up to five years
- HERMES – cover up to five years
- NAMUR – cover up to five years
- ECGD (used to be called Export Credit Guarantee Department) – with cover up to 10 years and more (from two years).

Insurance broking firms

There are also many insurance broking firms with specialist credit risk insurance divisions.

What brokers do is to assess the credit risk requirements and obtain premium quotations to suit the needs of the business you negotiated. It is important for you to know what risk you can insure against. Here are just a few important ones:

- insolvency of your customer

- buyer's failure to pay within six months of the due date for goods accepted

- buyer's failure or refusal to accept goods which comply with the contract.

There are also what are called **country risks** which you can insure against and you should seriously consider insurance in a number of circumstances, for example:

- difficulties or delays in getting funds out of your buyer's country

- intervention by government, preventing the contract being completed in full or part

- civil war or war outside the UK

- cancellation or non-renewal of an export licence or the imposition of new restrictions by the importer's country or an exporter – *eg* Libya.

What will you receive if you make a claim?
Insurers generally provide up to 90 per cent of loss cover, but a lower agreed percentage to cover, for example, manufacturing costs and maybe a proportion of the profit margin, could result in a lower premium.

Advice

● Count the premium as part of your costs when you come to fix the price.

● Do not dismiss the idea of credit insurance because you only export to countries which you do not think are likely to block transfer of funds to the UK. You never know what can happen overnight – by when it may be too late! That is why insurance is so important.

8
Getting Help with Language Training

Having a working knowledge of one or more European language will help you when trying to win business abroad. Exporters should consider providing language tuition as part of their company's training policy, and not assume that overseas buyers speak English.

ENCOURAGING YOUR STAFF TO LEARN ANOTHER LANGUAGE

If you have employees who have a language qualification from school, encourage them to develop it into a business language capability. It will be useful for any number of reasons. For example:

- for taking telephone calls from overseas
- for contacting overseas buyers in cases of need
- it creates an excellent impression when meeting or greeting overseas visitors
- letters could be translated, although anything more than simple letters will need expert attention.

You will probably have to use an interpreter in some countries. This is particularly so with technical or complex issues as you are seldom going to be able to work on a direct level yourself unless you happen to be a skilled, fluent linguist.

Tutoring your staff

There are a number or organisations who will tutor your staff but before you commission any training at all consider the following:

- Who needs to be trained?

- To what level do staff need to be trained?

- How much time can you afford people to take 'off' for training?

- Which language or languages do you need to have?

- Do you want 'in-house' training or training carried out at a centre?

- Do you want your staff to be assessed?

- What can you afford to spend or invest? Prices range from £25 to £50 per hour of contact time depending on the number of learners involved.

Then consider which system of training would be most appropriate.

Intensive language training
Intensive training is conducted over a period of one or more weeks for, specific purposes *eg* attendance at a trade fair or to brush up on existing language skills.

Extended language training
This is favoured by many organisations and involves weekly training, using multi-media packages such as books, computers, audio *etc.*

Individual or one-to-one training
This is the most expensive but most effective system of language training.

FINDING A GOOD LANGUAGE TRAINER

Approach the National Business Language Information Service (NATB-LIS) which is located at the Centre for Language Teaching (CILT) in London. This is a database of language training providers, holding information on other services such as interpreting, cultural briefing and language audits. This service is supported by the DTI.

You can also approach the Association of Language Excellence Centres, which is a network of centres established to provide language and export services for local companies. There are approximately 50 such centres throughout the country and the organisation recognises centres of excellence in foreign language training (LX centres).

There are also many top-rated private organisations but you should research them thoroughly before commissioning any work or courses and check whether they are members of a reputable training organisation or recognised professional body. Check also the experience and qualifications of the language trainers.

Ask the short-listed candidated companies to prepare a detailed proposal of the training they intend to provide and how it is to be delivered – together with their costing or charging structure – to include materials as well as time. Then interview their executives again before making a selection.

Extending your staff's skills

Language training should be seen as a **facilitation** enabling staff with *existing* business skills to operate more effectively in an international environment.

I*t will not turn people into fluent, professional lunguists* but it will help any motivated staff perform better and improve their career prospects.

And, if being able to converse, even haltingly, in another language helps win or keep hard-won business and orders, then the investment is worth every penny.

Case study
An engineering company based in the Midlands found that it was having no luck in winning orders from bids made for jobs in Italy, even though they knew that they met every aspect of the customer's specification, delivery date and price area. The Managing Director decided to have his sales manager trained to speak some basic Italian.

The result was that the manager enjoyed learning and speaking Italian so much that he won a considerable amount of new business from this particular prospect customer and began to take orders from other companies in the north of Italy as well. Although by no means perfect, his Italian impressed his customers who felt that a real effort had been made to address them in their own language.

Note
Western European languages can be learned to a fairly practical level in a few weeks. For Eastern European languages you must allow several months to become even adequate. With any Far Eastern languages you will probably need a minimum of two years, although this depends on the intensity of the course. Even so, even a modest conversation on a social level will be greatly admired and appreciated.

9
Importing

Many exporters are themselves importers in the first place, because they have to bring into this country raw materials, components or parts for assembly or finishing. When complete, the goods are exported all over the world.

Even if the goods are already complete on import for use in this country, executives in charge of this activity have an onerous task in ensuring that what is needed is bought at the best price, on the right terms, of the right quality and arrive when required.

Importers sometimes attract criticism for not acting in the best interests of their country because they spend precious foreign currency and do not support home-based industry, resulting in the closure of factories and increased unemployment. Unlike exporters, importers do not receive any government help.

However, the reality is that if Britain did not import, much of what we do export just would not happen, and if we did not buy from overseas, they would not have sterling to buy from us.

World trade is growing at a fast rate and it is forecast that within a few years the demand for shipping space will increase by around 70 per cent. Any advanced trading nation will need to know how importing works so that it can properly take advantage of this tremendous growth. It does not make economic sense to encourage inefficient local production by limiting or preventing imports. Nor does restricting the choice of goods for the consumer.

Consider this. Almost everyone in the world is both a seller and a buyer – so by buying you are allowing others to sell. So **importing** and **exporting** are interrelated activities.

BEING A BUYER/IMPORTER

Generally when you buy you are able to dictate the terms – if you do not like them you can walk away and go elsewhere. However this isn't the case if there is only one supplier of the kind of goods you require.

Examples

Oil
For years, OPEC countries have dictated the price and terms on which oil is supplied, even to insisting on receiving payment in US dollars. This almost bankrupted some countries which needed oil, but had no foreign currency.

Coffee
Brazil supplies a great deal of the world's coffee. Severe weather has in the past devastated the crop, pushing up world prices and sending buyers scurrying to other parts of the globe in search of the quality coffee they require.

Deciding what to import

Consider this. Manufactured goods make up some 50 per cent of all British imports, with an additional 15 per cent of food, drink and tobacco and 15 per cent of raw materials. The rest is made up of oil and other general items. Which products show most promise for the future? This is a question you must answer (unless you are buying for adding value) before you decide to import anything.

Here is a short list of items which you may like to examine:

- convenience foods
- drinks
- fashion goods and textiles
- toys
- vehicles
- electronic goods (all types)
- DIY products (home and garden).

This country is now importing many of what were traditional exports as other 'developing' countries are now producing these goods at better prices than ours. We therefore concentrate on more sophisticated products, although manufacturing is carried out under licence in some of these so-called developing nations, because labour is less expensive. The major suppliers of these products are:

- North America
- Japan
- Europe (even from former COMECOM countries)
- Hong Kong

- Malaysia
- Taiwan
- South Korea.

Many basic or raw materials come from Africa, and Central and South America.

Understanding legal aspects of importing

The legal position with regards to imports is that you are not allowed to import anything into this country without an **import licence** issued by the Department of Trade and Industry, Import Licensing Branch (see Useful Contacts) by reason of the Import of Goods (Control) Order. This applies to all goods apart from samples and goods for repair, and household goods if you are to be a resident in Britain. However, in practice, most goods are imported under what is called open general licence, although an entry permit is needed before HM Customs and Excise, who are responsible for all imports, will clear the goods.

Where you will need special licences is in the import of guns, drugs, plants and animals *etc.* So check with the DTI before you begin importing to ensure that you have the correct licence.

Apart from labelling and marking, you must also check the use of raw materials, ingredients, safety issues with which your suppliers and you will have to conform.

Customs and/or excise duties may have to be paid on goods coming into the UK and VAT will be charged where applicable, at the same rate as home or locally produced goods.

Importing indirectly

Using a wholesaler or import merchant
You can import via a **wholesaler** or **import merchant**. These traders bring the goods into this country and sell them to you. They assume all the risks, arrange insurance and transport and relieve you of all the documentation aspects. In effect this means is that you are buying in exactly the same way as you would if you were buying in the home market.

Benefit
Wholesalers/merchants often stockhold; they also sometimes specialise in products or trading areas. They are independent and can negotiate for best deals.

Using an import agent
You can import through the **import agent** of the overseas supplier and there are two types of these:

● *Commission agent* – who takes orders from you for his principal to deliver. The agent earns a commission for his reward and effort.

● *Distributor* – who buys stock from the supplier and sells to you and whose profit is the difference between his buying and selling prices.

Using a UK subsidiary of an overseas supplier
You can import through the **UK subsidiary of an overseas supplier**. This is the same as buying in the domestic market – no language documentation or currency worries! You do not even have to worry about quotas, tariffs, duties *etc.*

If you trade via any one of these systems you will pay a price for the convenience. Also you have very little chance of meeting the original supplier to negotiate any decent terms. To do this you really need to be the customer working directly with the exporter/ manufacturer.

Information about import merchants of all kinds is available from the British Importer's Association (see Useful Contacts).

Importing directly
In order to import directly you will have to find your own suppliers and negotiate directly with them. You should get much better terms leading to a higher profit level. But where do you find the right supplier?

● The Department of Trade and Industry keeps data of what is imported into Britain and its source for all products.

● Embassies, High Commissions and Consulates have commercial sections promoting their countries' products and can provide names of suitable suppliers.

● Many countries have Trade Councils which deal directly with UK importers – *eg* Ireland – who have the Irish Trade Board – and India, to name but two.

● In some countries, there are specialist trade organisations, for example British Overseas Trade Group for Israel, British China Trade Group.

- Chambers of Commerce are often contacted by overseas suppliers looking for UK importers.

- Major banks also receive enquiries from overseas from suppliers searching for new opportunities.

- Libraries contain useful trade information about suppliers in directories, trade journals *etc*.

- Trade shows held here in the UK are excellent opportunities to get to see and check on new products and suppliers on the spot.

- Many Trade Missions are sent into the UK from overseas to sell into the UK. Check with your local Chamber of Commerce for details of any such activity.

Most of the information available from the above sources is free.

As with exporting, it is always an excellent, even essential, idea to go and visit the market you are considering buying from and check the supplier, production and quality control, ability to supply your requirements *etc*. Do your homework first and go with a proper list of questions. If you are entering into a contract, make sure it is properly drawn up and fully understood. For example, if it came to litigation under whose law would it be judged? Check also the method of transport and decide who will arrange it.

Maybe your supplier needs an **export licence** – do you need an **import licence**? Are the goods you intend to bring in the subject of quotas? The Multi Fibre Agreement has a lot to say on fabric *etc* and quota restrictions can pose severe problems for importers. What about conformation to British or EU safety standards, marking, labelling *etc*?

Obviously you must check on the price and remember all the extra charges you, as the importer, may have to pay. What is included in the quoted price? Never assume anything! Which currency are you going to pay in? And by which method? What security will you have that the supplier will actually supply?

You must therefore decide whether to:

- import indirectly
- or import directly.

Then the crunch question is: *What are you going to do with the goods once you get them?*

DEALING WITH QUOTATIONS, ORDERS AND CONTRACTS

There are a number of factors which will affect the price quoted you by a supplier. These are:

● *When the order is placed*. No supplier wants to give a guaranteed price for more than six months ahead unless they are forced to in order to win and retain a contract. Mail order companies have particular needs, one of which is the requirement to have catalogues printed and distributed and for prices to be held. Therefore state clearly when you want or will be able to buy. If you buy immediately you will get a better price.

● *The quantity of the items/commodity to be bought*. The simple law of production says, in most cases, that the more of one item produced, the lower the unit cost. Even if three capital items are bought rather than one *eg* generators from Italy, you would probably be offered better terms for cash. You may expect **quantity discount**.

● *When and how to pay*. If you pay cash, you may get a discount; if you pay in German DM now, you will pay less than if you offer some other currency at a later stage. If your supplier does not want or need your business, he will quote unacceptably high prices, delivery dates far ahead of your schedule or lack of stock, production *etc*.

Advice on quotations

● Always identify yourself clearly and the ways in which you can be contacted.

● Tell the supplier what business you are in, what use you are making of the goods/commodity and where you sell; bank reference should also be given to convince the supplier you are *bona fide* and serious.

● Describe exactly what you want.

● Advise how the goods are to be packed and marked.

● Let the supplier know what quantity of goods you want.

● Inform the supplier when you will order and want delivery.

● Let the supplier have an idea of the terms on which you propose to deal.

● If you are going to arrange insurance and transport, advise the supplier.

● If there are any stipulations regarding the order which may be outside the normal conditions, tell the supplier.

● If you want all the transactions to be in English, again tell the supplier.

A **pro forma invoice** is the best way for a quotation to be made but:

- make sure it is signed
- make sure the signature is legible
- make sure you have the person's title.

Terms of delivery

In the section on exporting, the main **terms of delivery** were discussed and described. As a quick reminder, these are:

● *Ex-works* – where delivery/possession takes places at the gates of the seller you, the buyer, are responsible for transport and insurance.

● *Free carrier* – (named place) which could be positioned anywhere. This could be useful to small businesses once you are importing on a regular basis from different suppliers. The seller provides an export licence if needed and completes all customs documentation.

● *Free on board* (fob) – when the goods go over the ship's rail, delivery is effected and the buyer takes over responsibility. **Fob** is popular because it allows the buyer to nominate the carrier, which could save on foreign exchange.

● *Cost and freight* (C&F or cfr) – named port of destination, where the seller arranges to pay charges to the place of destination (ship/airport), but not the insurance, which is the buyer's responsibility.

● *Cost insurance and freight* (cif) – named port of destination, where the seller pays the insurance as well as freight charges. Only applies to sea transport.

- *Delivered Duty Unpaid* and *Delivered Duty Paid* (ddp) – named place of distribution. These are self-explanatory but you must still check that the seller has in fact cleared all the charges which he has accepted in his quotation.

You must decide which terms suit you best. **Ex-works** is usually the cheapest, with **delivered duty paid/unpaid** being the most expensive.

Note
Although most countries accept INCOTERMS from the International Chamber of Commerce for the quoted terms, the USA has different interpretations, so be on your guard and get a mutual understanding of what has been agreed.

Advice
Try and get a quotation in sterling and then pay in sterling, as you will always know what you have to pay when you have to settle the account.

Contracts and orders
When you come to place the order you must take great care to be absolutely clear of the following points:

- precise details of what is ordered
- quantity
- prices
- terms of delivery.

Make sure also, that you get an acceptance – under English law this is the first part of a contract.

Never assume anything – always ensure every detail tallies with your order. It is always best if you can have the contract subject to English/Scottish law. If not, you may have to adopt the Uniform Laws of the International Sale of Goods, which is the nearest there is to a worldwide law of contract.

Insurance
Much of the issue of insurance has already been covered in the section dealing with Exports.

There is no law which demands that goods and cargoes have to be insured but you would be wise to cover them against damage or loss. Depending upon the terms of trade, either you or your supplier will insure them.

Check these points and then decide what cover you need:

● The London Institute of Underwriters have produced *institute cargo clauses* A, B & C. The nearest to 'all risks' is **Clause A**, which does not mean you can cover illegal transactions! Nor can you insure against inherent vice, which means that some cargoes will inevitably suffer some harm because of what they are *eg* salt will attract water. You can however, add a special 'war' risk or even a special 'strike' risk – indeed, you can add almost anything you like to these Institute Clauses.

● *The period for which goods are covered.* The insurance will last from the time the goods leave the supplier's warehouse until they reach your warehouse. If they come by sea there is a period of 60 days *after* they have been unloaded during which they will be covered; by air it is for only 30 days after the aeroplane has been discharged.

● You must decide the value of the goods – *ie* the **insured value**. The minimum should always be the price quoted for the goods plus 10 per cent to cover the expense of putting you back to where you would have been had the loss or damage not occurred.

● If you import regularly, you may take out some form of **open cover**, whereby all shipments are automatically covered by underwriters, being declared to them after goods have been shipped.

If you are new to importing, the freight forwarder you work with will issue you with certificates of insurance from his own **open cover policy**. Later when you are more experienced, you may well handle the insurance yourself – and it may be cheaper to do so.

Making a claim for loss or damage
As soon as you discover any problem – or the goods fail to arrive – call in **Lloyd's** or the insurance company's agent to prepare a **survey report** which **certifies** the extent of any loss or damage. You must supply evidence that:

● the goods *are yours* via the invoice your supplier will have sent you

- the goods were indeed shipped via the bill of lading, sea waybill or container bill for sea freight or air waybill for air freight, convention internationale merchandises (CIM) for rail or convention merchandises routiers (CMR) for road transport (see page 146).

- the goods were insured in the first place

- letters have been written relative to the damage or loss to those likely to have caused or been responsible *eg* the carriers, handlers at ports *etc* for such damage or loss.

LOOKING AT TRANSPORT

If you leave transport in the hands of your supplier, for example by accepting the goods on **cif** terms, you will have to accept his estimate of the costs and accept the level of efficiency of the arrangements he makes. Even if you do accept **cif** terms, you still have to arrange for the goods to be unloaded and cleared through customs and taken to your own place of business.

If you buy **fob** (free on board), you will have to arrange transport and insurance in your supplier's country. In this case you would be well advised to use the services of a freight forwarder, many of whom have agents overseas and who can not only handle that part of the movement, but also help when the goods arrive in the UK.

As a small importer, it would make sense for a professional to look after your shipment using their own transport if they have it, or by grouping shipments – called 'groupage' – where the goods for the same destination are brought together, saving costs.

Freight forwarders charge a percentage of the *total freight costs* but the benefit to you is invaluable. After all, cargo movement and all that is involved is their business.

Always work closely with your freight forwarder and brief him thoroughly so that both parties fully understand what is required: the costs, the time factor and which documents are going to be needed. Not all freight forwarders are efficient, but this is often because they are inadequately briefed. Make sure that you understand as much as possible about the transport business so that you are able to give the freight forwarder all the information he needs.

If you need to find a good freight forwarder, contact BIFA (see Useful Contacts). This organisation requires that members provide a high-quality service, with evidence that experienced, qualified personnel are employed with adequate liability insurance cover. Not all freight forwarders are members.

Examining the methods of transport

As with exporting there are five main ways to have your imports brought into this country:

- sea
- air
- road
- rail
- post.

Sea

Most cargo goes by sea. It is slow, but cheaper than the other methods. There are however, no limits to size, weight or shape. Many shipping lines are members of a **conference**, which means that, just like a bus service, the times are guaranteed between two ports and the charge is the same whichever line you use. For a small importer, however, sea may not necessarily be the best method.

Air

Transporting goods by air is faster but more costly. Where speed is essential however, transporting by air is the obvious choice. Parts, medicines, fashion goods, flowers/vegetables *etc* will usually be flown in. As small quantities are often the norm for smaller importers, the cost/speed/quantity factor will not be so important.

Road

With the Channel Tunnel now taking a huge amount of rail and road freight, trucks and lorries can avoid the ferries and arrive quickly at their destination. Cheaper than air, with highly competitive rates, throughout Europe and the Middle East, road transport is a serious option, especially if freight forwarders operate their own transport and groupage arrangements. For those goods which do use the ferries, the **roll-on/roll-off** services make the cross-Channel or North Sea crossings relatively speedy. Smaller importers will no doubt have goods brought in via this system.

Rail

Although rail now makes delivery from anywhere in Europe very fast, small importers probably will not have much call on rail. Container services have speeded the turnaround times and rail companies are bringing in new services all the time to encourage more traffic. However, in comparison with road and air transport, rail's share of freight transport is very small. Main users are bulk commodity traders or large multinational companies which can negotiate special contract rates.

Post
For importers who purchase in small quantities and fairly frequently, then the post will be a good option as it does away with any problems associated with the other systems.

The post offices abroad will use air or sea to ship parcel post and here your goods will arrive at your door. The postman will even collect customs and VAT (where applicable) on small-value consignments up to a fixed amount. Provided that what you are buying can be accepted by the postal services, then this system could be the best and least worrying for you.

Examining the cost of transport

Sea charges
The shipping lines will charge you the rate applicable to your type of goods, to London or any other UK port from the supplier's port. This charge is based on a weight/volume ratio. You must have your consignment measured in centimetres and then convert this to cubic metres (divide by one million). You must then weigh the load in kilograms and convert the figure into metric tonnes (divide by 1,000). The larger figure will be the one used to calculate what you pay in freight charges – plus any extras. For example, if the cargo *weighs* two metric tonnes but *measures* three cubic metres. You will be charged *three times* the freight rate.

Remember – if you use a shipping (conference) line regularly, make sure you get a discount. Also be aware of the fact that freight charges are paid in advance, although if you use a forwarder this will be paid for you.

Rail and road charges
Rail and road charges are based upon the same weight/volume ratios. Rail charges are basically standard in Europe but, as mentioned, road charges are highly competitive.

Air charges
Air charges are similar throughout for all IATA airlines (non-IATA airlines have different rates) but the cost will relate to the type of goods and length of flight. Airlines work on a weight/volume ratio but this one is based on 7,000 cubic centimetres to one kilogram. As a result, charges relate to weight rather than volume.

Postal rates
Charges will have to be checked out with the post office/Royal Mail as
well as the maximum weights and dimensions.

Deciding which system is for you
You must make a decision based on:

● the type of goods you are importing (perishable, commodity,
fashion, consumer, durable *etc)*

● the quantities being imported at one time

● the urgency of your consignment

● the cost (speed equals cost initially but the speed may enable you to
sell the goods more quickly).

Finally, much may depend on how your supplier expects to be
paid. For example, if your supplier insists on being paid *before* you
take possession of the goods, he may say that the goods should go by
sea.

Packing and marking

● Specify any special packing that you know is essential to protect the
goods, whichever system of transport is being used.

● Make sure you do not pay for unnecessary packing (air packing is
less expensive than sea packing).

● Mark the goods with you own order number so that you can relate
packs to orders.

● Mark the goods with the destination port; if they are coming to you
in Watford via, for example, Southampton, mark them 'Watford via
Southampton'.

● Where there are, for example ten packages, number them 1 of 10, 2
of 10 *etc.*

● Use a mark for identification if you have one and have two lines
underneath.

● Never reveal the contents on the outside of the packages, but ask the supplier for a packing list.

Understanding the main shipping documents

Sea
The shipping line may issue to the shipper a **bill of lading** which you will need when you collect your goods. A bill of lading has three main functions:

1. It is a contract of carriage between the shipping line and the consignor.

2. It acts as a receipt for the goods by the shipping line.

3. It acts as a document of title to the goods.

The sea waybill and liner waybill
A sea waybill and liner waybill are not documents of title, therefore you do not need to have the actual paper to present to the carrier to take possession of your goods. Both act, though, as a receipt for the goods from the shipper and as a contract of carriage.

Air
The consignor will be given an air waybill which acts as:

● a receipt for the goods
● a contract of carriage.

But an air waybill is not a document of title. You will probably receive it after the goods have been shipped and all you need to know is the AWB (air waybill) number – because when you take delivery the goods will be stored and identified by their air waybill number plus the identity of the carrier.

Advice
Make sure your supplier faxes, telephones or EDIs (Electronic Data Interchange) the air waybill number because you may have some trouble when you go to collect your goods from the airport.

Road
The carrier issues a document which is the equivalent of the air waybill

– the **CMR** note, but this is mainly for the carrier's own use. A CMR (Convention Merchandises Routiers) is not needed for delivery as it acts only as a receipt for the goods and as a contract of carriage.

Rail
The equivalent document to the CMR for rail transport is the CIM (convention internatiole merchandises) note.

Post
When goods are sent to you via the mail, the packages must be accompanied by a properly completed customs declaration (check with HM Customs for full details) which gives in full the nature, quantity and value of the contents of each package.

PAYING YOUR SUPPLIER

You must first establish your creditworthiness with your overseas suppliers, who will be certain to check this before any contracts are negotiated.

When you send an order or a request for quotation make sure you give the name and address of your bank and ask your supplier to request a reference (or several). Like most banks, their response will be carefully couched so as to avoid any repercussions on them. The best thing to do is to have a discussion with them, especially if the sum you are seeking is a fairly large one or one that is larger than you would usually need.

As a buyer, always pay on the due date so that you establish a reputation for prompt payment.

Determining how to pay
As in exporting, for importers there are a number of ways in which you can settle what is due to be paid. Although you can decide what system suits you, the final choice may rest with the supplier who may set the terms.

There are a number of main methods of paying your overseas supplier (readers who have been referring to the section on exporting will see the same methods explained, but this time the situation is reversed).

Cash in advance
The supplier will be pleased to have prepayment, but from your point of view, this is the least satisfactory – on two counts:

- you rely on the honesty of the supplier to send the goods
- you are out of your money until you receive the goods and start selling them or adding value (processing) to them.

Try to avoid paying cash in advance if you can. However, some exporters will insist on advance payment so if this is the case bear in mind the following:

- send a cheque which will take time to clear, or send a banker's draft (but this may be stolen)

- send money via the **swift** system (computer based) which transfers money between banks in different countries

- ask for a sizeable discount which could equal the cost of the money during the period you are without its use.

Documentary letter of credit
About 20 per cent of the world's trade is conducted via a **letter of credit** because it gives you and your supplier some protection – you do not pay until and unless the goods and the money have both been vouchsafed by the banks concerned. Letters of credit work like this:

- As a buyer you open a documentary letter of credit through your bank in favour of your overseas supplier.

- This clearly states how much you are prepared to pay, when and, vitally, under what conditions you are prepared to pay.

- You know then what you are going to be committed for.

- Your supplier knows that he will be paid.

Having laid down the terms and conditions, you instruct your bank to open a credit in favour of your overseas supplier and you tell your bank that it is:

- **Irrevocable** – which means that it cannot be altered without both parties' agreement

- **Confirmed** – which means that your (UK) bank will ask the seller's bank in his country to confirm payment to the supplier. Your bank sends this bank the credit to allow this to happen.

Warning
Avoid **revocable** letters of credit, and always make sure that they
are **confirmed**. (The various types of letters of credit are more
fully described in the section on exporting.)

Once you have instructed your bank you must satisfy them that you
have enough funds for the credit to be paid when it falls due. The next
stages are as follows:

1. The seller's bank will be advised that such funds are available and
   the bank is then able to tell your supplier of the situation. He will be
   asked to confirm all the details of the credit as you have worded it.

2. If all is in order, then the supplier will ship the goods.

3. The documents relating to the sale will be sent to his local bank who
   sends them on to your bank so that you have the right to take
   delivery.

4. As soon as this stage is reached and the supplier's bank is happy
   that the documents are what you expected, the supplier will be paid
   the full amount of the credit.

Basically, the banks act as go-betweens and references ensuring that
not only the goods and money are exchanged, but also that all the
documents relating to the consignment are present and accurate.

Caution
If the supplier wants you to change some or any of the conditions laid
down, it is up to you whether you do or not. If you make changes the
bank will charge you extra, on top of what it cost to open the credit in
the first place. Therefore, try and get it right first time. Many importers
have found their margins squeezed by incurring avoidable bank charges
relating to letters of credit.

Bill of exchange
You may wish to pay once the goods have arrived or even later, giving
you time perhaps to sell the goods and so recover the money you need
to pay for them.
   A bill of exchange is a demand for money for goods/services

supplied. Here is how a bill of exchange works from the importer's point of view:

- Your supplier, having shipped the goods, will draw a draft (a bill of exchange starts initially as a draft, becoming a bill after acceptance) on you.

- The draft is sent to the supplier's bank with all the shipping papers and requests his bank to have the draft presented to you by a bank here in the UK.

- This UK bank will present you with the draft and hand over the documents which will permit you to take delivery of the goods *provided* you paid or accepted the draft. There are two types of draft – sight and term. These are self-explanatory, as sight drafts are payable at sight, term being paid after so many days after sight – normally 30, 60, 90 days up to 180 days.

- With a payment on sight draft, you get documents and the goods.

- If you receive a term draft you write 'accepted' on it, sign it and receive the documents and the goods but pay later. The draft is now a **bill of exchange**.

- Your bank remits the proceeds to the supplier's bank and the circle is complete. This is a good deal for you because you have time to pay – but not so good for the supplier: not only has he sent the goods but he is not totally certain he will be paid!

Again, trust has to be shown on both sides – to release documents for you to take the goods and for payment when due. Failure to pay a draft when due could wreck your credit rating and could result in a court action.

Note
If a draft is drawn in the importer's currency, it will be paid at the current rate of exchange for drafts payable in the UK – rates quoted daily by the banks.

Open account
The bulk of world trade is conducted on **open account**, which means that you buy from and pay your overseas supplier in much the same way

as you would from a domestic supplier with whom you deal on a regular basis. This means you pay some time after you receive your invoice from the supplier.

Purchasing from European suppliers is not normally made on receipt of invoice but usually against a document similar to a bill of exchange (which is a demand for payment) so that an actual payment date is agreed. If you do not have a draft drawn on you, you can instruct your bank to transfer funds by **swift** to your supplier's bank.

Consignment stock

This is akin to goods on 'sale or return'. If you buy from overseas you will be reluctant to pay for them as you have no notion what will sell. You take them on **consignment** meaning that you do not take title to the goods but you distribute them (and sell them).

You pay nothing until they are sold and you have been paid. Not a very popular measure, even with domestic companies, it is even less popular with overseas suppliers. Payment to the supplier is via **open account**.

Countertrade

The various forms of countertrade have been covered in the export section of this book. As a small or new importer, unless there are really good commercial reasons for becoming involved, it would be wiser either to avoid countertrade deals altogether or to seek the advice of a factor specialising in countertrade who could handle the complexities of such a deal on your behalf.

Foreign currency and exchange

Usually as an importer you will only be able to pay your overseas supplier in sterling because that is our currency at the moment. We cannot pre-empt the ECU or Single Market currency, so while this eventually may cover EU members, there will be other currencies with which importers have to trade or work in. Some importers may have special accounts held in dollars or deutschemarks *etc* which are used to pay for imports, but for the most part smaller importers will use sterling.

If you pay in your own currency you will have to get it changed into your supplier's currency and you do this on the foreign exchange market. You may be fortunate in that your supplier has quoted you in sterling (see export section, Chapter 7), so you have no need to buy any foreign currency, leaving this aspect to your supplier to deal with when he receives your sterling payment.

If you pay in sterling you know exactly what you are going to have to pay – as per quotation – but if you are quoted in another currency, you stand the risk of the exchange rate going against you when you come to settle. *Never* gamble that the exchange rate will move in your favour – you are trading in goods not currencies!

Avoiding risk in currency fluctuations

If you accept quotations and place orders in your supplier's currency and you agree to pay in that currency (some organisations demand payment in US$), you need to lay off the risk of loss on the foreign exchange. You do this by making a contract with your bank which you must honour, but which will ensure you do not lose, no matter what happens to the exchange rate between the two currencies.

Forward exchange contract

This is where you guarantee to *sell* the sum you owe for the goods in sterling to the bank on a certain day (or between certain dates in the future) and to *buy* the equivalent amount of your supplier's currency so that you can pay him with it.

Your bank will agree the rate of exchange at which the deal will be struck and they will stick with this rate whatever happens to the rate later. You will then know exactly what you are going to pay and you cannot lose on the exchange, so you have no risk to bear.

Advice

Consult your bank about forward exchange contracts, which are available in all major currencies for periods of up to six months. You then apply the forward rates to your orders and the agreed method of payment.

Benefit

You can cost in properly all the charges which are attached to the financing of the transaction. You can then arrive at a selling price in the UK, knowing that your margin will not suffer due to fluctuations in the currency markets.

Working out the cost of money

Your money will be tied up for some time before you have recovered the cost of purchases and paid your supplier. How can you work out what the costs are?

Example

Assume that the cost of borrowing money is 10 per cent per annum and you buy £1,000 worth of goods, with payment due in 90 days (before you receive the goods). The formula you use is:

$$\frac{90 \times 10}{365} = 2.465\%$$

ie multiply the number of days' credit (90) by the rate and divide by the number of days in a year. Turn this into a fraction = $\frac{1}{40}$.

Deduct one figure from the lower number = $\frac{1}{39}$, and if you apply this to £1,000 you get £25.64, which is the cost to you of being out of £1,000 for 90 days. Always bear this cost factor in mind when calculating your total costs, which will include other items such as handling goods, documentation charges *etc*.

Advice

● *When* you pay will affect your costs and this should be used as a bargaining point with your supplier, and normally the longer you have to pay the better.

● Where possible *you*, as the importer, should take the initiative and decide on the method of payment which best suits you.

10
Dealing with Import
Regulations and Controls

OUTLINING IMPORT REGULATIONS

All imports, just like exports, need to be checked, controlled or regulated for economic, social, financial or political reasons. Sometimes governments impose stiff controls or limits on certain imports because of the need to protect home-based industries and thereby jobs.

The aim of all signatories to the **General Agreement on Tariffs and Trade (GATT)** and the aim of the **World Trade Organisation (WTO)** is to liberalise trade by reducing tariffs and other barriers to trade, such as import quotas, use of foreign currency and specially imposed regulations (*eg* special exhaust systems on imported cars into the USA and Japan).

There are now trading blocs in the world – the EU is one, the North American Free Trade Association (Canada, USA and Mexico), EFTA (European Free Trade Association) and others – the aim of which is to allow simpler trading between members.

As a member of the European Union, Britain allows most goods from other member states into the country free of customs duty – because they are deemed to be of Community origin *ie* wholly obtained within the Community or produced there from imported materials and parts, provided that all duties were paid on such goods when they entered the Community and no duty is reclaimed when re-exported. The goods are declared to be in 'free circulation' – and no customs duties are paid on them.

Note
Excise duty is still payable though, which is charged on imported and home-produced goods at the same rate.

Example
Wines and spirits would come into this country free of duty from France but the excise duty would be delivered on French brandy at the same rate as on a bottle of Scotch whisky. VAT is also payable as it is on UK goods.

Advice

Check with HM Customs and Excise (see Useful Contacts) for details about tariffs, quotas and preferential regulations, rules of origin, duties payable *etc* because these change regularly; also check which documents you will need, if the exporter has not provided them or advised you, to enable the goods to enter this country and under which terms.

Checklist

Here is a checklist of points which should help you with your enquiries:

● Is there any duty to pay on the goods?

● If so, is there a reduced duty level?

● Are there any limits to what can be imported – *eg* the EU imposed quota restrictions at a moment's notice on the import of Chinese silk to 'protect' European manufacturers. Companies who had contracted for supplies months ahead suddenly found that their orders would not be admitted, causing enormous confusion and financial problems for importers.

As a small or new importer you will probably only be concerned initially with a few goods from limited sources – so ask for Customs to give you the regulations covering them, and follow the information provided.

UNDERSTANDING IMPORT CONTROLS

Having briefly looked at import regulations, it is important to understand some of the basic import controls.

An import licence is needed before any goods may be brought into the UK, apart from:

● trade samples and printed trade advertising material
● goods returned for repair
● personal and household effects
● gifts
● private cars
● goods returned to the UK after being hired for use overseas.

Where do you obtain import licences? From the Import Licensing Branch of the Department of Trade and Industry (see Useful Contacts).

In most cases the procedure is a formality with most goods being imported under what is called an **open general licence**, which means that you do not have to apply for an import licence – but you must check to see if your imports fall within this general category.

If you do need an import licence, it may be one of three kinds:

● **Open individual import licence**, which means that you can bring in specified goods without limit on quantity or value from a stated source for a period of time (or until revoked).

● **Specific import licence**, which is for a stated period and value for imports from a nominated source.

● **Surveillance licence**, which will be needed for all goods subject to the EU's surveillance licensing restrictions which come into the UK from beyond the EU countries.

Every import licence has an expiry date by which time the goods must have been imported. Extensions are not automatically granted so, if you need an extension, you will have to go back to the Import Licensing Branch before the goods leave your supplier and tell them in detail the reason(s) for the delay.

Note
There are five categories of goods which need to have the country of origin marked on them:

● textiles
● clothing
● footwear
● cutlery
● electrical appliances.

When these goods are advertised to retail customers, their country of origin must be clearly stated and you must avoid using any brand name which could cause confusion with an existing British brand name.

Clearing your imports through Customs
HM Customs and Excise has the right to inspect goods at any time and will want to see any relevant import licences. Not only do they wish to stop smuggling, they also need accurate data on what is being imported so that trade data covering exports and imports can be accurately

compiled showing or assessing the country's balance of trade. You or your freight forwarder are responsible for clearing your imports through Customs and this involves:

● payment of any port charges

● preparation of Customs documents and payment of Customs duty

● payment of any local transport charges

● arrangements for insurance to cover your goods.

Knowing about shipping documents

In most cases your supplier will supply the shipping and other documents but you should know what these documents cover, because there may be times when you might want to arrange for the despatch of goods to your warehouse yourself. Even if you pass the job to your freight forwarder you should at least know the documents which are commonly used for the shipment of goods from one country to another.

Invoice

This, as already mentioned elsewhere, is not a demand for payment but a record of goods sent plus evidence of a contract.

If your supplier has despatched the goods, he must also show details of the freight and insurance as separate items. Invoices supplied by the supplier must be certified as correct as regards the value and origin of the goods. You will need extra copies for HM Customs – check how many in advance.

Certificate of origin

Although **a certificate of origin** is not especially needed, you will want this document when preferential rates of duty are being claimed, issued and signed by a Chamber of Commerce in the supplier's country.

Packing list

A **packing list** is basically a 'common-sense' document itemising what is in the package. It could be useful for insurance purposes.

Transport documents

Transport documents have been well covered in the section on transport and include a bill of lading or air waybill, CMR or CIM note. You will need the air waybill if you collect your goods from the airport but in all other cases (road, rail or air) you will not need the air waybill, CMR or CIM to obtain delivery as the goods will be sent directly to you.

Import licence
You may need a special **import licence** depending on what you are bringing in – if it is needed, you must attach it to the other shipping documents when the goods are cleared on arrival.

Movement certificate
Movement certificates are important if the goods are entering this country at **preferential rates of duty**. If they are, then you should ask your supplier to send you one of the following:

● Certificate of Origin for Goods Entitled to the Generalised System of Preferences (GSP) Form A (see Figure 10)

● EUR 1 or EUR 2 for Preferential Trade Agreements (PTA) goods (and for Spanish territories – Canary Islands, Ceuta and Melilla)

● an invoice declaration or an EUR 1 for goods coming in from an EFTA country (Iceland, Norway and Switzerland).

Whichever one of these forms is used it must be signed before they are shipped – and in some cases by the local Chamber of Commerce in the exporter's country.

Certificate of insurance
A **certificate of insurance** will be needed, of course, in the event of any claims you make relating to the condition (or loss) of the goods on arrival. The certificate must show:

● value of goods
● the risks covered by the insurance
● your endorsement (clearly).

This document has to be included in the documents required when trading with a letter of credit. Although there are other documents used in shipping, the ones listed are the main documents. You will find that, if you are dealing with animals or plants or agricultural products, you will need health certificates and test and inspection certificates for others. Check with both HM Customs and Excise and the Import Licensing Branch as to what is required.

<table>
<tr><td>1 Consignor</td><td colspan="2">No. FH 237181</td><td>ORIGINAL</td></tr>
<tr><td rowspan="2">2 Consignee</td><td colspan="3">EUROPEAN COMMUNITY</td></tr>
<tr><td colspan="3">CERTIFICATE OF ORIGIN</td></tr>
<tr><td></td><td colspan="3">3 Country of Origin</td></tr>
<tr><td>4 Transport details (Optional)</td><td colspan="3">5 Remarks</td></tr>
<tr><td colspan="3">6 Item number; marks; numbers, number and kind of packages; description of goods</td><td>7 Quantity</td></tr>
</table>

8 THE UNDERSIGNED AUTHORITY CERTIFIES THAT THE GOODS DESCRIBED ABOVE ORIGINATE IN THE COUNTRY SHOWN IN BOX 3

THAMES VALLEY CHAMBER OF COMMERCE & INDUSTRY

Place and date of issue; name, signature and stamp of competent authority

. . . . 19

. . . .
Thames Valley Chamber of Commerce & Industry

DTI/XP 13026

Regent Print Group, Huddersfield

Fig. 10. Certificate of Origin.

Sometimes your supplier will want to know that the goods did actually arrive in this country, in which case you can get, from HM Customs, either a **delivery specification** or **verification certificate**.

Receiving documents
How you pay affects the timing of the despatch and receipt of the documents.

● If you pay by **cash in advance** the documents (two sets usually) are made out to you and sent by air.

● If you pay on **open account** the same procedure is followed.

● If you pay by **letter of credit** you will receive the documents only when all the details have been thoroughly checked to ensure that all the conditions have been met. The advising bank will then forward the documents to your bank who send them on to you or your import agent/forwarder.

● If you pay on a **bill of exchange** (draft), all the shipping documents will be sent to the exporter's bank who sends them on to a UK branch, who presents you with the draft.

Note
Drafts are payable at sight or at a later date. If you pay on sight you receive the documents from the bank as you pay. If it is paid at a later date, you receive the documents when you accept the draft.

Advice
Even if you leave the paperwork to your forwarder or import agent, you should try to know about and understand the documents you are likely to need, how they are to be made out and how many copies are required and where they go.

DEALING WITH DUTIES OR RELIEFS

Informing HM Customs correctly
You have to present correct information to HM Customs and it is solely your responsibility – or your import agent's – to do so if goods imported attract any duties. You have four options.

● You intend to pay the duty in full and take the goods.

- You claim relief, either by:
  - **duty suspension,** whereby duties are not paid on arrival but a bond is given for their security, or
  - **reimbursement,** whereby duty is paid on importation but is repaid on re-export after successfully claiming relief.

- You can store goods in a **bonded warehouse** without payment of duty. They are under Customs control and remain there until they are either re-exported or entered for home use on payment of the relevant duty. This means that you pay duty on only what you actually draw from the warehouse and avoid tying up a lot of capital as a result.

- You can store the imported goods in one of the many new **freeports** dotted around the country. This has the same advantage as a bonded warehouse. No duties are payable when goods enter and they can leave 'as and when'. Manufacturing can take place with a freeport. Customs duties are only payable when goods actually *enter* the country for (re)sale or when entering another country after leaving the freeport.

Customs will demand an **entry,** the type of entry depending on the end use of the goods – so it is vitally important for you to have all the details of your shipment ready and accurate so that duty can be assessed.

HM Customs have enormous powers and can check shipments at random or for a particular reason. If they feel that their **revenue** is being denied then they can:

- ask for duty to be paid there and then
- retain the goods
- ask for a bond or cash deposit which will cover the maximum duty payable. This will be refunded or adjusted when the final entry is agreed.

Note
Customs 'entries' may be lodged at the relevant Customs office up to four days prior to the arrival of the ship or aircraft and up to seven days after by air and 14 days later if coming by sea.

Finding out the rates of duty
To find out what rates of duty you will be charged, consult the Customs' Tariff and Overseas Trade Classification published by HM Stationery Office, now a privatised body.

There are basically two categories of duty:

● **Fiscal charges** – these are excise duties charged on imported goods at the same rate as for domestically made goods.

● **Customs duties**, and agricultural levies arising from the Common Agricultural Policy (CAP). The main Customs duties are **specific** and *ad valorem*:
  – **Specific** – is a charge of a set amount per unit or net weight or other agreed measurement of quantity detailed in the tariff.
  – *Ad valorem* – is according to the quayside value of the goods.

Note
There are a number of special charges and rebates relating to items such as tobacco, beer, matches and hydrocarbon oil. Check with HM Customs Notice 320 for up-to-date information.

Understanding how Customs interpret value
Value, according to Section 258 of the Customs and Excise Act 1952, is based on what is called **open market** concepts, which is the price the goods would fetch when Customs accept 'entry' for home use on a sale between buyer and seller, where the seller bears all the costs relating to the sale including delivery to the buyer.

This does become rather complicated when dealing with reliefs granted to EU members as well – also dependent upon where in the EU the goods were valued in the first place, as goods coming into, say, Southampton via Le Havre could be valued in Le Havre even if duty is to be paid in Southampton.

***

Advice
Get to know the reliefs you can rightly claim for your range of product or goods because such reliefs will make an enormous difference to the way you can trade.

***

Case study
A major UK aircraft manufacturer buys items from all around the world. The sums involved run into hundreds of millions of pounds sterling. Because the chief buyer and his staff understand minutely all the reliefs available on each product or part, from each country, he is able to save tens of millions of pounds in duty, either by not paying it in the first place or by recovering it later. If such attention to duty and the

appropriate relief were not paid, the result for the company in a recent year would have revealed a loss rather than a profit, plus loss of cashflow and resulted in borrowings.

Although smaller importers are not working on such a scale, the study illustrates that it is important that you and your agent know what is recoverable or avoidable, and how to process your goods and paperwork to get relief from duties.

Dealing with VAT on imports

VAT is charged on all imported goods – regardless of whether you are registered for VAT. (VAT is not levied on imported *services* though.) *All registered businesses* pay VAT on imported goods *at the time and place of entry*. It can be reclaimed in due course and, of course, VAT can be claimed back on some goods *eg* those which have been re-imported without having undergone any change or because they have been only temporarily imported. If in doubt check VAT notices 700 0702.

Understanding tariff preference quotas

Most developing countries can export goods to this country on a preferential duty basis – which means that less duty is paid on them when coming into Britain.

Goods coming in from least developed countries attract no duty at all. However, for trade-sensitive items this treatment is limited by quota which means that when the UK preferential import duty quota is exhausted, the full rate of duty becomes payable.

The quota limits for each country are administered separately, with the exception of certain handmade products from countries where the quota is treated globally.

For details of the tariff quota system, you should ask HM Customs and Excise for Part II of their tariff – but you can also get information from the Central Tariff Quota Unit of the International Customs Division, (see Useful Contacts).

To obtain proper benefit of the preferential rate of duty, you must make sure your supplier sends you the right **certificate of origin** – but to be eligible for preferential duty the quota works on a first-come-first-served basis until the quota is exhausted.

Note
Your goods may arrive in this country when the tariff quota is exhausted. In this case you can store the goods in a Customs warehouse and so avoid paying the full duty. However, you will have to weigh up the storage costs against the duty to be paid to see which course of action is best.

Advice
You will find that HM Customs and Excise offices are extremely helpful, so never hesitate to consult them for clarification of any point relating to duty, preferential rates, tariff quotas *etc.* However, apart from any duty you may eventually have to pay, there are other costs involved in getting goods through Customs.

CLEARING GOODS THROUGH CUSTOMS

The best advice that can be given about clearing goods through Customs is to use a good freight forwarding agency, who not only knows all about moving goods in and out of this country and others, but also knows about dealing with Customs.

You should consult either *Yellow Pages* to locate one in your vicinity or approach the BIFA (whose details are given in the Useful Contacts section) who will nominate suitable and qualified members for you to approach.

Most exporters and importers seem to be fazed by Customs clearance procedures but as long as you work with and learn from a good freight forwarder, the system is not really that daunting.

Understanding what information Customs requires
You need to provide the following for Customs:

● the **Customs Procedure Code** (CPC) – is a six-digit number which identifies whether the goods are for home use or processing for future export

● import licence details, if any

● name/address of importer

● consignor's name/address

● place or port of importation, place of discharge or unloading

● nationality and name of ship/airline

● where the goods were loaded overseas

● an exact description of the goods

- the **Customs Tariff Number** – which, under the Harmonised System of Classification, explains what the product category is for duty purposes

- the quantity being imported

- the country of origin

- the country from whence the goods were consigned to you

- the value of the goods for Customs purposes

- the duty payable – showing any preferential rates of duty claimed

- special surcharges or even rebates

- who is paying any Customs duty

- consignment marks/numbers

- number and description of the packages and number in words

- bill of lading or air waybill number

- the number of any duty deferment approval

- liability for VAT and VAT registered number.

You will also have to provide a number of supporting documents – the most important one being C105A or 105B, which are used for goods liable for *ad valorem* duty and valued over £1,300.

Note
When you become a regular importer, you should know that you can make a general valuation statement on Form C109 instead of lots of forms C105. When you become really large, you can import through the CHIEF system (Customs Handling of Import and Export Freight) and use yet another form – C106.

You are not yet complete! Further information is required:

- evidence of carriage *eg* the relevant transport document

- the freight charges paid on **fob** goods

- extra copies of invoices if part of a consignment is entered elsewhere

- your authority as importer to your agent to make declarations for you

- overall worksheet covering several invoices or tariff items entered

- a delivery verification certificate (proof of receipt for the supplier).

And finally:

- original invoice plus copies

- packing list

- specifications where necessary

- certificate of origin (for preferential treatment) or Form A

- a movement certificate for goods entitled to enter the UK under preferential rates of duty.

Advice
Spend time getting all the documents and ensure their accuracy –
otherwise you will pay full duty.

What happens next?

You take the Customs entry and all supporting documents to the **long room** of the Customs House at the port of discharge (remember the specified period depending on method of transport) and you will usually wait 24 hours before goods can be collected, having paid the relevant duty and VAT charges.

Then your original entry will be sent to the Customs officer at the docks for comparison with the details listed on the Master's report. If everything is in order, an **out of charge note** is issued and the goods are released. Importers may like to know about some procedures which could help them.

- Triplicate entry procedure used for perishable goods at airports which have no **long room** facilities.

- At most airports there is a **Transit Shed Register** (not Heathrow or Gatwick) which is used for clearing items up to a certain value (check with your freight forwarder what this value is). This means you do not have to complete all the usual entry forms.

- There is also a **Simplified Procedure for Import Clearance** for goods of low value.

- The **fast lane** is designed for goods imported by short sea routes *eg* France, Belgium, Holland, where entries can be processed before the goods arrive.

The documentation of imported goods has been greatly simplified and only the bare bones of what small importers need to know about has been covered. While you should know something of the process for bringing goods into this country and through Customs for clearance, the real answer is to work closely with a good freight forwarder who will relieve you of most of the day-to-day paperwork, leaving you to get on with your task of negotiating, selling, marketing, distributing *etc.*

Attention to the various aspects of importing as discussed in this book will help you import more efficiently, hopefully more profitably. With experience and by working with a good freight forwarder, you will realise that importing, just like exporting, can be rewarding.

Glossary

AAD. Accompanying administrative document. This is a document that accompanies goods sent to EU destinations from another EU country where excise duty is payable. It enables Customs to keep a check on the cargo until duty is paid.

Act of God. A concept in English law which relieves the common carrier of liability for losses suffered as a result of events so unusual as to seem to be the result of some supernatural power.

Ad valorem. Literally 'according to value', a method of charging freight or Customs duty on high-value goods.

Agent. Works on commission only.

Air waybill. This is a document made out for the carriage of goods by air. There are 12 copies of which the most important are the three signed copies – one for the consignor, one for the carrier and one for the consignee. Most are now computer generated – at least in the UK.

Avalised bill of exchange. A guarantee of payment because the avalising bank is a party to the arrangement (signed by the bank itself).

Barter trade. (Including countertrade, compensation, counterpurchase, offset and switch trading) – a system by which goods rather than money are used as the medium of exchange. Sometimes both goods and cash are used.

Bid or tender bond. A legal document in substitution for *earnest money* issued by tenderer's bankers.

Bill of exchange. A method of payment in both inland and foreign trade. Learn its definition by heart! 'A bill of exchange is an unconditional order in writing, addressed by one person to another, signed by the person giving it, requiring the person to whom it is addressed to pay on demand or at a fixed or determinable future time, a sum certain in money to, or to the order of, a specified person, or to bearer.'

Bill of lading. This is a document made out in the carriage of goods by sea. It acts as a receipt for the goods shipped, is evidence of the terms of the contract of carriage and is a quasi-negotiable document of title to the goods.

Bonded warehouse. A warehouse for goods stored under Customs control pending payment of duty. In the EU they are called tax warehouses.

Cabotage. The practice of reserving internal or coastal traffic to national flag carriers.

Carnet. A pad or set of international transport documents as used in TIR (Transport International Routiers) transport to provide two copies for every frontier crossing.

Certificate of origin. A document certifying the place of growth or manufacture of an article for export. The certification is done for a fee by a chamber of commerce on proof of the true facts about production.

CHIEF. A mnemonic for Customs Handling of Import and Export Freight. It is a new computer system which replaces DEPS.

Common carrier. A carrier who holds himself out as ready to carry for the public at large. He is liable for every loss that occurs apart from five common law exceptions: act of God; act of the Queen's/King's enemies; inherent vice; and fraud of the consignor.

Conference. An organisation of shipowners engaged in the same trade which sets a common tariff and enters into contracts with shippers.

Confirmed credit. A letter of credit issued by an importer's foreign bank which has been sent to its correspondent bank in the exporter's country with a request that the exporter be notified of the existence of the credit and that the correspondent bank confirms it – which means it has to pay the exporter without any recourse in the event of non-transfer of funds from the issuing bank.

Confirming house. An export organisation which buys goods for foreign customers, guaranteeing payment to the exporter at once and thus 'confirming' that the order is from a reputable customer.

Consignee. Receiver of goods.

Consignor. Sender of goods.

Consular invoice. An invoice, prepared on a special form and validated by the consul of an importing country, vouching for the legality of the transaction and its conformity with the rules of the country re origin, value, price *etc*.

Credit reference agency. An agency which keeps records on those who borrow money, buy goods on hire purchase or order goods with a view to paying later. It will also interview such firms, examine records and report comprehensively on the risks involved.

CRN. Customs registered number – a number allocated to an exporter or freight forwarder for use when exports are to be entered under SCP (simplified clearance procedure).

Del credere. (In the belief that) – a name given to an agent who receives extra commission in return for agreeing to bear bad debt risks.

Distributor. Buys and sells in his own right (principal to principal).

Documentary credit. A major method of payment in international trade whereby payment is made available at a bank and will be released against the surrender of specified documents which comply with the letter of credit.

Drawer. The person who writes out or draws the bill of exchange. The 'drawer' calls upon the drawee to pay the sum due on demand or at some fixed or determinable date. Until the drawee accepts the bill of exchange the drawer is the only person liable upon the bill.

Earnest money. A percentage of the tender price showing evidence of tenderer's seriousness in bidding.

ECGD. Export Credit Guarantee Department (now privatised) – this department covers commercial and political risks for non-payment for goods/services on long-term contracts (over two years at least).

EDI. Electronic Data Interchange – an electronic system for transferring structured data from one computer to another (or several). The system can be accessed by authorised parties.

Export house. A commercial house which specialises in making purchases for foreign customers and in exporting goods.

Export licence. The DTI issues such licences for the export of items over which control is exercised.

Factoring. Term used when you sell your debtor receivables.

Forfaiting. Term used to 'discount' or 'forfait' bills of exchange.

Forward rates. For deals to be done at some time in the future. These are spot rates either at a premium which will be lower than the spot rate, or at a discount, which means that they will be higher.

Freight forwarder. A good freight forwarder will not only ship your goods from factory to recipient, but also handle all the relevant paperwork/documentation.

Frustration. The termination of a contract as a result of a major event which prevents fulfilment *eg* war or an illegality, vessel sinking.

General average. A method of compensating those who make a sacrifice (goods, ship or money) to save the entire venture in perilous marine situations.

Groupage. A system of consolidation used to obtain the benefit of cheaper rates for full loads.

Harmonised system. The name for the Customs co-operation system for deciding codes for commodities passing through ports.

House air waybill, house bill of lading. Documents issued by an air forwarder or freight forwarder to recognise the grouping of consignments in a groupage operation.

ICC. International Chamber of Commerce – promotes world trade. Paris based.

ICD. Inland clearance depot – defined by HM Customs as a place approved by them to which goods imported in containers may be removed for entry, examination and clearance; equally, where goods for export can be made available for export control.

INCOTERMS 1990. A set of 14 internationally agreed terms of trade whose definitions of buyers' and sellers' duties are made clear.

Invoice. A business document made out whenever one party sells goods or supplies services to another. It is written evidence of a contract and may be produced in court.

LEC. Local export control – a system of clearing goods through Customs at exporter's own premises.

Manifest. A summary of all bills of lading, sea waybills, non-negotiable receipts and parcel receipts loaded on a vessel. Nowadays they are transmitted by EDI to recipients.

Multi-modal transport. (MMT) – a system whereby goods are moved by the most economical transport system door to door. Easy transfer from one mode to another is essential – containerisation being ideal.

Noting. The act of noting on an inland bill of exchange the failure of a party to accept the bill on presentation for acceptance or to pay when due.

Open account trading. The least secure method of payment – but by far the most common, relying on the buyer to pay you on an agreed basis.

Pro forma. A specimen invoice which, if acceptable to the recipient, may become the basis for a firm contract.

Quasi-negotiable instrument. (Quasi is Latin for 'almost') – while a bill of lading can be assigned to a third party by endorsement, it is not fully negotiable since it only passes on the same title as the giver of it.

ROC – Return on Capital. Management must assess the overall performance of a firm. The appropriate measure for corporate performance is the return on stockholders equity. This is measured as net corporate profits as a percentage of the equity capital in the firm.

NB: Although profitability is most important it must be remembered that management establishes other criteria as well. Sales, market share, capital and investment ratio, and the marketing expenditure and sales ratio are frequently used as criteria to evaluate performance.

Ro/ro ship. A roll on/roll off vessel enabling vehicles to drive on and off.

SAD. Single administrative document – Customs declaration for both import and export cargo, introduced in 1988. Not now necessary for intra-Community trade, it has residual use for certain goods and is still important for non-EU trade.

SCP. Simplified clearance procedure – exporters of goods not requiring special control may submit an abbreviated pre-entry on an approved commercial document to Customs at the time of export and provide the full statistical information within 14 days after the goods are exported.

Sea waybill. This is a non-negotiable document made out to a named consignee and, providing the latter can give proof of identity, he may claim the goods from the carrier without producing the sea waybill.

SITPRO. Simpler Trade Procedures Board – the UK representative on international panels designed to simplify international trade by the development of aligned documentation and EDI systems.

Spot rates. Rates for deals concluded on the spot.

SSN. Standard shipping note – a six-part document which accompanies goods to the customer's base or dock and acts as a receipt for goods to the road haulier.

T-form procedures. The EU transit document procedure which not only indicates to Customs officers the status of goods in the EU, but which, provided their seals are unbroken, also enables vehicles to cross frontiers without inspection. Effective more for non-EU goods.

WTO. World Trade Organisation – body set up to ensure trade barriers of all kinds are reduced or abolished and that competition is fair. Promotes world trade as well.

Useful Contacts

Association of British Chambers of Commerce, London. Tel: (0171) 222 1555. Fax: (0171) 799 2202. Coventry. Tel: (01203) 694484. Fax: (01203) 694690.

British Exporters Association (London). Tel: (0171) 222 5419. Fax: (0171) 222 2782.

British Franchise Association (Henley on Thames). Tel: (01491) 578049. Fax: (01491) 573517.

British Importers Association (membership body), contact Chris Starns. Tel: (0171) 258 3999. Fax: (0171) 724 5055.

British International Freight Association (BIFA). For details on freight forwarders. Tel: (0181) 844 2266.

Business Links (DTI Small Firms Section) Sheffield. Tel: (0114) 259 7549. Fax: (0114) 259 7540.

Central Tariff Quota Unit of International Customs Division, King's Beam House, Mark Lane, London EC3R 7HE.

COFACE, London. Tel: (0171) 325 7500. Fax: (0171) 325 7699.

Customs Statistical Office, Southend-on-Sea. Tel: (01702) 348944.

European Commission Office, London. Tel: (0171) 973 1992. Fax: (0171) 973 1900.

Export Buying Offices Association (EXBO), London. Fax: (0171) 351 9287.

Export Licences, London. Tel: (0171) 215 8070.

HM Customs and Excise (Head Office) London. For general enquiries Tel: (0171) 626 1515 or (0171) 620 1313.

Institute of Export (membership body), London. Tel: (0171) 247 9812. Fax: (0171) 377 5343.

International Union of Commercial Agents & Brokers (Amsterdam). Tel: 00 206 221944.

London Chamber of Commerce and Industry. Tel: (0171) 284 4444.

NAMUR, Croydon. Tel: (0181) 680 1565. Fax: (0181) 688 4953.

Overseas Promotion Support (DTI). Tel: (0171) 276 2414. Fax: (0171) 222 4707.

Patent Office and Trade Marks Registry, Newport, South Wales. Tel: (01633) 814000.

SITPRO (Simpler of International Trade Procedures Board – making your import/export documents easier to understand and operate). Tel: (0171) 215 0825. Fax: (0171) 215 0824.

Training and Enterprise Councils (Business Counselling, Consultancy Support – Department of Employment & Education) London. Tel: (0171) 273 6969.

Credit risk insurers

NCM, Cardiff. Tel: (01222) 824000.

ECGD (Export Credit Guarantee Department) London. Tel: (0171) 512 7000. Fax: (0171) 512 7644. Cardiff. Tel: (01222) 784000. Fax: (01222) 784448.

Hermes Credit Services, London. Tel: (0171) 600 4406. Fax: (0171) 600 4426.

Department of Trade and Industry

Country Desk. Tel: (0171) 215 5000 and ask for the country desk required.

Duty Remissions Branch, London. Tel: (0171) 215 5000.

Export Market Information Centre (EMIC). Tel: (0171) 215 5444/5. Fax: (0171) 215 4231.

Export Marketing Research Scheme (EMRS). Tel: (01203) 694484.

Import Licensing Branch, Billingham, Cleveland. Tel: (01642) 364333.

Freight Forwarder

Frazer International, Unit 7, McKay Trading Estate, Blackthorne Road, Colnbrook, Slough, SL3 0AH. Tel: (01753) 682322. Fax: (01753) 686027.

Language training

DTI Languages for Export. Tel: (0171) 215 8146/4857.

CILT. Tel: (0171) 379 5131. Fax: (0171) 379 5082.

Association of Language Excellence Centres (Manchester). Tel: (0161) 228 1366. Fax: (0161) 236 8667.

Pre-shipment agencies

Cotechna International Limited, Hounslow, Middlesex. Tel: (0181) 577 6000.

SGS, Camberley, Surrey. Tel: (01276) 691133.

Reporting agencies

CCN Systems Limited, Nottingham. Tel: (01159) 863864.

Dun & Bradstreet Limited, High Wycombe. Tel: (01494) 422000.

INFOCHECK, London. Tel: (0171) 377 8872. Fax: (0171) 247 4194.

Index